MW01092720

More Praise for *The Positive Organization*

"Few argue with being positive, but fewer can turn aspirations for being positive into specific organizational actions. Quinn is an exquisite observer and advisor on organizations. This book specifies actions that leaders can take to create abundant or positive organizations. The ideas make sense, the tools are informative, and the examples are clear. This book lays the foundation for redefining organizations."
—**Dave Ulrich, Rensis Likert Professor, Ross School of Business, University of Michigan, and Partner, The RBL Group**

"A profound book offering wise lessons for igniting deep positive change in your organization. Sound too good to be true? Actually, I think it may be an understatement. *The Positive Organization* can help you discover the vision and practices needed for creating cultures of possibility where people exceed expectations and flourish in their work."
—**Charles C. Manz, coauthor of *Share, Don't Take the Lead* and *Self-Leadership***

"Bob Quinn addresses the practical realities of building a positive enterprise and the positive culture necessary to sustain it."
—**Bill Robertson, Chairman, Weston Solutions, Inc.**

"Ten years ago I read *Building the Bridge as You Walk on It* by Robert Quinn. It changed my career. As I read his new book, I realize it is having the same kind of impact but at an organizational level. I have already started applying the ideas to my company, and the results have been powerful. If you want elegant, easy to access, and deeply engaging, start reading now."
—**Nick Craig, President, Authentic Leadership Institute, and coauthor of *Finding Your True North***

"Another insightful, poignant, and practical guide by change master Robert Quinn, *The Positive Organization* is the ultimate user's manual for leaders who want to create positively deviant organizations. It will work for people who want to change any organization, from a multinational company to neighborhood association."
—**Jim Mallozzi, Chairman and CEO, Prudential Real Estate and Relocation Services (Retired)**

"People are drawn to the positive. When we are engaged and creative, we are living for a greater purpose. But because we biologically defend ourselves above all else, the default in organizational life is being defensive and then infecting everyone around us with negativity. Quinn unveils the positive organization without being gushy or Pollyanna. He provides hope for the entangled, a spotlight to guide the lost, and reassurance for those on the journey."
—**Richard Boyatzis, Distinguished University Professor, Departments of Psychology, Cognitive Science, and Organizational Behavior, Case Western Reserve University, and coauthor of *Primal Leadership***

"Another masterpiece from Robert Quinn! I have worked with organizations on creating more positive organizations, and while everybody endorses the concept, people typically find it challenging to make it practically sustainable. Bob's new book provides valuable new examples that illustrate how to do this and tools to achieve success."

—Anjan Thakor, John E. Simon Professor of Finance, Director of WFA Center for Finance and Accounting Research, and Director of Doctoral Programs, Olin Business School, Washington University in St. Louis

"This is a wonderfully persuasive, tactile immersion in positive organizations that demystifies them and makes them more attainable while magnifying the reader's desire to get on with that attainment. This is Bob at his best! And it is positive organizing in its best rendering."

—Karl E. Weick, Rensis Likert Distinguished University Professor of Organizational Behavior and Psychology, Emeritus, Ross School of Business, University of Michigan

"Bob Quinn identifies the critical path to invigorate the human spirit at work. His daring description of being 'fully engaged and continually renewed' charts a course on how to invite people to the new possibilities of authentic conversations that ignite positive cultures."

—Jim Haudan, author of *The Art of Engagement*

"Who doesn't want to be part of an organization where people flourish, are unified with clear purpose, and exceed expectations? Robert Quinn's newest work offers clear pathways for leaders to authentically engage others, consider new possibilities, and think beyond problem solving. Building and understanding positive organizations helps create places where others want to contribute, results are celebrated, and people prosper. This book matters."

—Jim Mahoney, Executive Director, Battelle for Kids

THE POSITIVE
ORGANIZATION

OTHER BOOKS BY ROBERT QUINN

Deep Change: Discovering the Leader Within

Change the World: How Ordinary People Can Achieve Extraordinary Results

Lift: Becoming a Positive Force in Any Situation

The Best Teacher in You: How to Accelerate Learning and Change Lives

THE POSITIVE ORGANIZATION

BREAKING FREE FROM CONVENTIONAL CULTURES, CONSTRAINTS, AND BELIEFS

Robert E. Quinn

Best-Selling Author of *Deep Change*

Includes the Positive Organization Generator of
100 unconventional practices from real organizations

BK

Berrett–Koehler Publishers, Inc.
a BK Business book

Berrett-Koehler Publishers, Inc.
1333 Broadway, Suite 1000
Oakland, CA 94612-1921
Tel: (510) 817-2277 Fax: (510) 817-2278 www.bkconnection.com

Ordering Information
Quantity sales. Special discounts are available on quantity purchases by corporations, associations, and others. For details, contact the "Special Sales Department" at the Berrett-Koehler address above.
Individual sales. Berrett-Koehler publications are available through most bookstores. They can also be ordered directly from Berrett-Koehler: Tel: (800) 929-2929; Fax: (802) 864-7626; www.bkconnection.com
Orders for college textbook/course adoption use. Please contact Berrett-Koehler: Tel: (800) 929-2929; Fax: (802) 864-7626.

Distributed to the U.S. trade and internationally by Penguin Random House Publisher Services.

Berrett-Koehler and the BK logo are registered trademarks of Berrett-Koehler Publishers, Inc.

Printed in Canada

Berrett-Koehler books are printed on long-lasting acid-free paper. When it is available, we choose paper that has been manufactured by environmentally responsible processes. These may include using trees grown in sustainable forests, incorporating recycled paper, minimizing chlorine in bleaching, or recycling the energy produced at the paper mill.

Library of Congress Cataloging-in-Publication Data
   Quinn, Robert E.
   The positive organization : breaking free from conventional cultures, constraints, and beliefs / Robert E. Quinn, best selling author of Deep change.—First Edition.
     pages cm
   Includes index.
   ISBN 978-1-62656-562-3 (hardcover)
   1. Corporate culture.   2. Organizational change.   I. Title.
   HD58.7.Q56 2015
   658.3008—dc23   2015011093

First Edition
23 22 21 20 19 18   10 9 8 7 6 5 4 3

Cover/Jacket Designer: Crowfoot Design
Interior Illustration: George Whipple

I am indebted to a woman who breaks convention while living with discipline. I am grateful to have her as my loving daughter and the demanding manager of this book project. I dedicate this volume to Shauri Quinn Dewey and thank her for her endless, positive impacts on my life.

▲ CONTENTS

▲ INTRODUCTION

The Reality of Possibility

One day, Laura Morgan Roberts spoke at the Center for Positive Organizations. Dr. Roberts is a researcher who studies identity and seeks to understand how people can flourish at work. She spoke of modern work-life, the effort to find balance, and a terrible paradox she has identified. She pushed her clicker and a very simple slide went up on the screen. It read as follows:

Overextended and Underutilized

I could feel something happening. I looked around. The audience was full of professionals who work in organizations. The slide seemed to have an actual physical impact. Faces were full of pain. It was a rather remarkable moment.

Many people are overworked. They live on the edge of exhaustion. This fact is publicly recognized, and there is endless discussion about how to better manage our ever-shrinking supply of time.

What is not so widely recognized, however, is that many of those same people are being underutilized. Their strengths go untapped, and their unique gifts go unexpressed. They are giving all their time and energy, yet they get back only a financial return. Their paycheck is important, but it is not enough. As they pursue recognition, wealth, and security, they are infected by the epidemic of disinterest and end up joining the legions of the walking dead. Laura's slide seemed to bring all this to the fore in three simple words.

The next morning I found myself pondering Laura's paradox. Recognizing that every coin has a flip side, I wrote this contrasting paradox:

1

Fully Engaged and Continually Renewed

While the first paradox suggests a cycle of depletion that is not easily broken, the second suggests a cycle of renewal that is not easily believed. When I show these two contrasting paradoxes to people, they immediately identify with, and emotionally react to, the first. They see its negative message as both real and inevitable. It is a downward cycle that always threatens organizational life.

People react differently to the second paradox. They see it as an unreachable ideal. It is not something they experience or expect to experience. They believe, with good reason, that full engagement and continual renewal is not going to happen. Few people can envision it and even fewer ever aspire to creating such a reality. The lack of vision and aspiration is crucial to this cycle.

The Book

Your current organization is not static. It is continually becoming more negative or more positive. As organizations become more negative, the people within them tend to withdraw and underperform. As organizations become more positive, their people tend to invest and exceed individual and collective expectations.

The purpose of this book is to help create the second kind of organization. It not only illustrates how this is done in real organizations but also explains how to invite people to purpose, how to bring about authentic conversations, how to connect people to new possibilities, how to orient them to the common good, and how to facilitate the emergence of new, more positive cultures.[1]

The appendix contains a useful tool called the Positive Organization Generator. It includes 100 positive practices from real organizations. It is designed so the reader can create new practices that can be implemented in any context without having to ask for permission from someone of higher authority.

At the end of each chapter, you will be asked to think about a key insight you gained and how it can help you to create a more positive organization. It is important to follow through on this, because it will help you envision the organization you want to create as you use the Positive Organization Generator.

There are also other tools for readers. At the end of chapters 3 through 7, there are assessments and activities you can use to introduce your unit or team to the concepts in this volume.

In the end, this book does two things. First, it introduces ideas designed to challenge your conventional assumptions. Second, it offers real tools and simple processes designed to support you in trying new things.

Deep learning can occur when both challenge and support are present. As you begin to conceptualize new practices and to see things from a more complex mental map, you will be able to transform yourself, your unit, and even your organization. If that happens, you and your people will never be the same. Your people will begin to flourish and exceed expectations. They will become fully engaged and continually renewed,[2] and a more positive organization will emerge.

Acknowledgments

This book is full of stories. They come from the lives of wonderful people trying to make the world a better place. I am grateful for the legions of folks who have shared their life experiences and invited me to the wisdom of positive organizations.

In writing this book, there has been an effort to make it as accessible as possible. Much of the academic work that informs this text appears in footnotes. I am indebted to the scholars I cite. I am particularly indebted to the scholars and leaders who surround me at the Center for Positive Organizations. These include Wayne Baker, Kim Cameron, Jane Dutton, Betsy Erwin, Fred Keller, Shirli Kopelman, David Mayer, Roger Newton, Gretchen Spreitzer, Chris White, and Lynn Wooten. I am grateful to Erin YaLe Lim, my research assistant, who found most of the hundred practices in the Positive Organization Generator.

Many people have read some or all of this manuscript and made comments prior to publication. A large subset of them put more into the process than I have seen before. I am deeply indebted to Kirk Blad, Wally Bock, Bruce Degn, Dan Duckworth, Erin Dunn, Wade Eyerly, Kathleen Flanagan, Maria Forbes, Ed Francis, Mirena Hine, Jessica Johnson, Lucie Newcomb, Craig Matteson, Valerie Matteson, Ryan Quinn, Shawn Quinn, and Shuryce Prestwich. Thank you for your every expression.

I owe special thanks to Katie Outcalt and Mark Templeton. They read multiple iterations of the manuscript, sent extensive feedback, and continually challenged me to think more deeply.

In 1986, a young editor nurtured me through the production of my first book. His influence was extraordinary. Decades have passed, and now he is CEO of one of the most positive organizations in the publishing industry. Yet, he once again took on the difficult role of supporting me and pushing me forward in the creation of something that matters. I am forever indebted to Steve Piersanti and the entire staff at Barrett-Koehler Publishers. It is an honor to be associated with such extraordinarily constructive professionals.

Finally, there is Shauri. In launching this book, my daughter and I agreed on a bold experiment. She would become my manager. While living in the Republic of Georgia and raising a new baby, she threw herself into the task. There were daily phone calls in which she demanded that each page be rewritten, multiple times. The manuscript teems with her creativity and discipline. In gratitude, I dedicate this volume to my amazing and energizing daughter. Thank you.

Ann Arbor, Michigan
February 2015

1 ▲ THE POSITIVE ORGANIZATION

One day, I was talking with a young surgeon whose academic specialties included evaluating hospital performance. He thinks very deeply about what factors increase or decrease a hospital's effectiveness, and we were discussing how successful hospitals function. In the middle of our conversation, he paused and then surprised me with a question: "Why do people in finance so often end up as heads of organizations?"

This question caught me off guard, and I improvised some answers. I told him economics is a potent discipline, and people who master it have precise analytic tools. As they move up in their organizations, they learn to rigorously evaluate the allocation of resources in the system. By the time they reach the highest levels of the finance function, they have great skills for controlling an enterprise.

A commonly held belief in business circles is that people in economics and similar analytic disciplines know how to solve important technical problems and how to efficiently utilize resources. Therefore, they can keep things under control.

My friend nodded, but not with enthusiasm. He expressed some reservations about people who base their leadership on control, problem solving, and efficiency. I was not sure what was on his mind. So I asked him to elaborate, and he told me two stories. Each one was about leadership and culture in a hospital setting.

Two Hospitals, Two Cultures

The first story begins when my friend went with a team of colleagues to visit Hospital 1 and were warmly greeted at the front door by a man in a top hat. Inside, they saw the usual information desk and waiting area but also spaces available to the community for such things as weddings and cooking classes. As they toured the hospital, they got the impression this hospital was like a five-star hotel.

On their tour, they happened to bump into Hospital 1's CEO, who welcomed them and asked if he could help them in any way. He chatted with them for a half hour and shared his vision and philosophy.

During the rest of the tour, they asked the employees about the CEO. People at the lowest levels talked as if they had a personal relationship with the man. They also spoke with pride about the vision and values of the hospital. Clearly, people were unified and felt good about what they were doing. Their every word and action seemed to convey that they were fully committed to the hospital's success. There was a positive culture that seemed to focus, unify, and animate them.

My friend and his associates left deeply impressed. While they were all doctors who have spent their lives in hospitals, it was clear that they had just observed a hospital that exceeded their expectations. They had just encountered a truly "positive organization."

Shortly thereafter, my friend was dropped off at the front door of his own hospital: we'll call it Hospital 2. Given his recent visit to Hospital 1, he began to think about contrasts between that organization and his own. He then experienced one of the differences.

As he walked in, he was met by a gruff woman who wanted to know if he was a student. He explained that he was a surgeon and was scheduled to operate. She would not grant him entry, citing hospital policy. He would have to go back out and walk around to the employee entrance. The surgeon tried to handle the situation artfully, but the woman threatened to call security. He went back out.

A few days later, he related what had happened in a meeting with a senior officer of Hospital 2. This person responded to the story by asking for the name of the woman. The executive wanted to fire her.

My friend told me that this particular senior officer put a lot of emphasis on being in control and fixing problems. His first inclination, for example, was to terminate the troublesome woman. He assumed that she was "the problem."

To the administrator's mind, firing the woman was the right thing to do. He wanted to establish and maintain order and control. He wanted to make the hospital run better. A person who seeks a predictable, smooth-running organization often focuses on disruptions and disruptive influences: the natural inclination is to fix those disruptive problems. In this case, the knee-jerk solution was to fire the woman.

When we focus on a problem, we are not seeing the whole system. We are paying attention to something within the system. Likewise, when we focus on a single person, we are not focusing on the culture of which that person is a part. The aforementioned senior executive did not stop to wonder what systemic conditions within the culture might have caused the woman to behave as she did. It did not occur to him that if he fired the woman, the problem might not go away. The next person in the same role, responding to the same culture, might eventually behave in the same manner as this woman had.

When people focus on the part rather than the whole, it does not occur to them to ask a most important question: How might the entire culture be reshaped so the people flourish in their work and exceed expectations as they perform?

This book is about creating more positive organizations. The preceding question reflects the simplest definition of a positive organization.

> IN A POSITIVE ORGANIZATION, THE PEOPLE ARE
> FLOURISHING AS THEY WORK. IN TERMS OF
> OUTCOMES, THEY ARE EXCEEDING EXPECTATIONS.

To flourish is to grow and thrive. To exceed expectations is to successfully do more than people expect you to do; it is to move toward excellence. Hospital 1 had a culture of excellence. The young surgeon and his colleagues entered Hospital 1 with similar assumptions about what a hospital is like. During their visit, those assumptions were challenged. The surgeons saw people were flourishing and exceeding expectations. They saw a hospital that was performing at a high level because it had a positive culture. The surgeons had seen something that created dissonance in the way they viewed the world. Now they would have to decide whether to disregard it as an anomaly or examine that information more closely.

Mental Maps and Culture

Like the surgeons, all of us have a set of assumptions or beliefs that help us navigate the world we live in. These beliefs are acquired over time from the people we live with and work with. We learn from these people

7

and from our own experiences what works and what doesn't. These assumptions and beliefs then become like maps in our minds that guide our responses to what we observe and experience around us.

Our mental maps guide us in all areas of life: they create our picture of what family life is like. They tell us what to expect in areas like education, religion, and recreation. Because our assumptions are a product of our experiences, we take our beliefs as truth and seldom doubt them. We hold them tightly, and we tend to deny messages that challenge them.[1]

The mental maps we hold influence our approach to, and our beliefs about culture in our organization. In my experience, there are a few common ways that managers tend to think about culture. Group one, "The Discounters," ignore the fact that culture exists, and they often completely overlook or discount its impact. Group two, "The Skeptics," recognize that culture exists, but they have tried to make change, failed, and then incorrectly concluded that the culture is unalterable. Since experience doesn't lie, "The Skeptics" "know" that aspiring to excellence is both unrealistic and impractical.

Finally there are the few "Believers." These managers have also experienced organizational constraints, but they know culture change is possible because at some point they have tried and succeeded. In succeeding they learned something important. Instead of seeing the culture as a fixed constraint, they see it as the key to success. They recognize that their job is to lead culture change so as to create a more positive organization.[2]

Managers in all three of these groups carry a conventional mental map. We call this map conventional because it is guided by normal or common beliefs. For example, one conventional belief is that stability, hierarchy, and control are the keys to running an efficient and profitable business. There is truth in this conventional belief, so that map can be useful. However, when the conventional map is used alone, it can actually become a constraint. It can prevent people from pursuing the creation of an organization in which people flourish and exceed expectations.

The rare supervisors, managers and executives that fall in to the group of "Believers" have an advantage. They accept the conventional map and all of its very real beliefs and constraints, but they have also acquired a positive mental map. The positive mental map allows them to see possibilities that "Discounters" and "Skeptics" cannot see. They see the constraints and possibilities simultaneously, which allows them to do things the others cannot do. In chapter 2 we refer to this advantage as being a bilingual leader.[3]

Defying Conventional Culture

In the young surgeon's story from the beginning of this chapter, Hospital 2 appears to be led by people who only hold the more conventional or common mental map. I had the opportunity to work on a project designed to elevate over 60 nursing units in Hospital 2. We worked with the directors of the nursing units, dividing them into small groups and spending a week with each group to help them see how they could better empower themselves and their people.

The work proved to be a great challenge. It seemed that each time we surfaced some positive practice that might improve a unit, one of the directors would explain why it was impossible to employ it. They spoke of administrators who were punishing, doctors who were insensitive, policies that were inflexible, peers who did not cooperate, and employees who just wanted to do their job and go home. Experience taught these directors of nursing that the organization's culture was constraining. They did not expect the people in their units or people in other parts of the hospital to flourish and exceed expectations.

As we sought to modify their beliefs and elevate their aspirations, we began to examine the nursing units more closely. We looked, in particular, for a positive exception, a unit that defied the conventional culture of the hospital. The exception existed and was easy to find. When we asked administrators if there was such a unit of excellence, they all answered in the affirmative and named the same one, which I will call Unit 5.

Unit 5 served children who were seriously ill. This was demanding work, and yet they were usually first or second on every hard performance measure. Measures of morale were also high. In many of the other units, turnover was high; in this unit, however, the turnover rate was close to zero, and there was a long list of nurses waiting to transfer in. Why?

Other units in the hospital also served populations like Unit 5, but none performed like Unit 5. They seemed to take a unique approach to everything they did. Earlier in the hospital's history, for example, every unit had been given money to hire a hostess to greet new patients. Nearly all the units hired a nurse. Unit 5, however, hired a drama major and then sent her to clown school. When very sick children and anxious parents arrived on the unit for the first time, a very skilled clown greeted them. Within minutes, they felt they had become part of a special community in which they would be treated as full human beings.

When we interviewed the nurses in Unit 5, they told stories of people going the extra mile to take care of patients and each other. They spoke of collaboration and achievement. It seemed to be a place of high commitment and compassion.

The people we interviewed spoke of the unit director in the same way the people in Hospital 1 had spoken of their CEO. It was common for them to express extreme gratitude for the director of their unit. In our interviews, some nurses actually shed tears as they spoke of their leader. Their descriptions suggested that she was deeply committed to creating a positive unit in a conventional hospital.

The Reality of Constraint

Most organizations tend to be like the more conventional Hospital 2, where many of the nursing units were disempowering places. A few empowering exceptions are found, like Unit 5, but it is not the norm.

Recall that we found Unit 5 because we went searching for a unit of excellence, a positive exception in the organization. We wanted to challenge the tightly held assumptions of the nursing directors by exposing them to a positive reality within their system. We hoped to jolt their beliefs and open their minds to the possibility of thinking in a new and more empowered way.

What we learned is this: the directors, like many people in positions of authority, do not aspire to have flourishing people in their units. They instead seek to meet the minimum assumed requirement in order to survive. Survival, not flourishing, is the aspiration of conventional managers. They do not look for or expect to find excellence. When they do find excellence, they tend to ignore it rather than examine and learn from it. Everyone knew about the excellence of Unit 5, but it never occurred to anyone that it was possible to use that success as a lever for creating a more positive culture in other such units. The conventional focus on *constraint* precluded a focus on *possibility*.

Across the world, supervisors, managers, and executives learn to speak in politically correct ways about improvement. Yet, it is quite common for them to operate from a perspective of problem solving and task accomplishment. Perhaps it is natural, and even rewarded, for many of them to slough off any sense of responsibility for creating positive organizations.

> This book invites each one of us to become aware of the assumptions that form our individual mental maps (what we believe), how those maps guide our responses to what we observe and experience (our behavior), and how our responses create and reinforce the cultures we live in. It invites each of us to begin to become leaders who imagine and pursue the construction of positive organizations even amid the reality of constraints.

Expanding Our Mental Maps

We can begin to increase our awareness of the assumptions we carry in our own mental maps by understanding that organizations are not static. Human beings tend to use fixed, either/or categories. An organization is either positive or negative. Reality, however, is far more complex and more dynamic than that. Reality often runs across our logical categories. Although I have seen some organizational cultures that are quite negative or quite positive, I cannot imagine an organizational culture that is 100 percent negative or 100 percent positive. Nor can I imagine one that stays fixed in terms of negative and positive. What may be a weakness this month, may turn into a strength next month.

Hospital 1 appears to have a more positive culture than Hospital 2 but that doesn't mean that Hospital 2 is a "bad" organization. Hundreds of people leave that hospital each day healed of their diseases and injuries. Researchers generate scientific breakthroughs that change medicine forever. Leaders at many levels initiate projects to make things better. We even find the very positive Unit 5. Likewise, it is possible that in Hospital 1 we might find one or more negative units.

Negative and positive indicators, or behaviors, tend to appear in an organization at the same time. The ratio of positive to negative behaviors we observe tends to shape our assessment of an organization. For instance, in Hospital 1 and Unit 5, we see many patterns that exceed our conventional expectations, and we conclude that the culture is positive.

In trying to create a more positive organization there are many characteristics we could focus on. Here we have created a list of 20. Look at the first set of 10 and think about what value is placed on them in your organization.

1. Growth Focus: Growth mentality, investing in the future, seeing possibility
2. Self-organization: Empowerment, spontaneity, self-organization
3. Creative Action: Responsive, up-to-date, a learning organization
4. Intrinsic Motivation: Meaningful, rewarding, fulfilling work
5. Positive Contagion: Positive emotions, optimism, enthusiasm
6. Full Engagement: Committed, engaged, fully involved people
7. Individual Accountability: Responsibility, accountability, excellence
8. Decisive Action: Speed, urgency, decisiveness
9. Achievement Focus: Achievement, accomplishment, success
10. Constructive Confrontation: Honesty, challenge, confrontation

An organization with these 10 characteristics is likely to be very visionary, very productive and filled with people who could delight in achievement and success. Yet the careful reader might have some misgivings. The reader might recognize that a focus on a value like achievement could be coupled with human exhaustion, and an emphasis on growth and change could lead to waste, chaos, and confusion. That is because *every* positive characteristic, without a competing positive value or characteristic, can become a negative. With that in mind, let's look at 10 more characteristics.

11. Cost Control: Efficiency, conservation, preservation of assets
12. Organizational Predictability: Stability, order, predictability
13. Procedural Compliance: Sound routines, policies, procedures
14. Managerial Control: Consistent, dependable, reliable performance
15. Objective Analysis: Objectivity, measurement, sound analysis
16. Life Balance: Renewing, reenergizing, life balance

17. Cohesive Teamwork: Collaboration, belonging, positive peer pressure
18. Group Deliberation: Participation, involvement, consensus
19. Authentic Relationships: Caring, selfless service, genuine relationships
20. Appreciative Expression: Appreciation, praise, celebration for others

The second list is not an arbitrary set of items. Each characteristic balances the first list of 10. Please compare the first characteristic on the left with the first on the right, and so on, down the list.[4]

Consider some of the contrasts. Growth focus is very different from cost control. People who believe in organizational predictability may not see how a characteristic like self-organization is possible. Creative action and procedural compliance are also conceptual tensions or oppositions.

We use words like tensions or oppositions and not opposites because the word opposite often implies that two words or phrases are mutually exclusive. In fact, many people will look at the above lists and think that the pairs are mutually exclusive.

Although these characteristics appear to be opposites, they can exist simultaneously (and successfully) in the real world. In fact, they must exist simultaneously. Change and stability are positive tensions. If there was zero stability the organization would cease to exist. If there was zero change the organization would become completely unaligned with the internal or external marketplace. Customers or clients would become dissatisfied, and they would make their displeasure known in one way or another. External resources like money and political support would cease to flow, and the organization would eventually die.

The fact is that organizational success is dependent upon the integration of contrasting or paradoxical tensions such as the ones illustrated in the above lists. F. Scott Fitzgerald once said, "The test of a first-rate intelligence is the ability to hold two opposed ideas in mind at the same time and still retain the ability to function."[5]

One reason that we see so few positive organizations and so many conventional organizations is because of the tension between these necessary positive characteristics. Leadership requires the ability to hold opposed ideas at the same time. It requires us to think in more complex and adaptive ways.

First List	Second List
Growth Focus: Growth mentality, investing in the future, seeing possibility	Cost Control: Efficiency, conservation, preservation of assets
Self-organization: Empowerment, spontaneity, self-organization	Organizational Predictability: Stability, order, predictability
Creative Action: Responsive, up-to-date, a learning organization	Procedural Compliance: Sound routines, policies, procedures
Intrinsic Motivation: Meaningful, rewarding, fulfilling work	Managerial Control: Consistent, dependable, reliable performance
Positive Contagion: Positive emotions, optimism, enthusiasm	Objective Analysis: Objectivity, measurement, sound analysis
Full Engagement: Committed, engaged, fully involved people	Life Balance: Renewing, reenergizing, life balance
Individual Accountability: Responsibility, accountability, excellence	Cohesive Teamwork: Collaboration, belonging, positive peer pressure
Decisive Action: Speed, urgency, decisiveness	Group Deliberation: Participation, involvement, consensus
Achievement Focus: Achievement, accomplishment, success	Authentic Relationships: Caring, selfless service, genuine relationships
Constructive Confrontation: Honesty, challenge, confrontation	Appreciative Expression: Appreciation, praise, celebration for others

Figure 1.1 is an unusual tool because it makes us conscious of something that is usually ignored: the tensions that exist in all organizations. Figure 1.1 can help us recognize where our organization is and where it is that we want it to go.

Holding two opposed ideas is challenging, but let's go one step further. Figure 1.1 illustrates the 20 positive characteristics discussed above, along with the 20 negative characteristics that can develop when we give a positive characteristic too much attention. You will see that each pos-

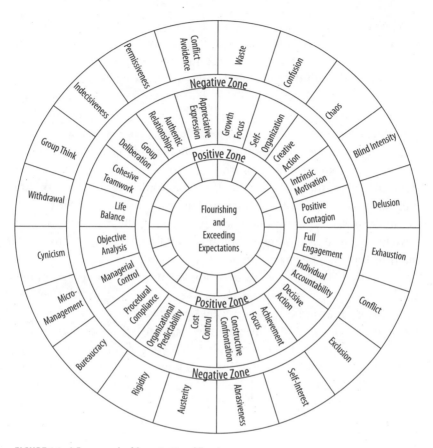

FIGURE 1.1 A Framework of Organizational Tensions

itive is linked to a negative. Not only do we need the ability to accept two opposed ideas at the same time, but we must also give each of these competing values enough attention so that neither one crosses the line and becomes negative.

> In building a positive organization the first challenge is to see the organization not as a static entity, but as a system of tensions. The second challenge is to see all the tensions and not just the ones we are trained to see. This means we have to see the whole system. The third challenge is to realize that positives like full engagement can turn into negatives like exhaustion. The task is to hold the dynamic system in the positive zone of Figure 1.1.

By way of example, we expand the notion of full engagement and exhaustion. Withdrawal, life balance, full engagement and exhaustion run in a line across Figure 1.1. Life balance and full engagement can be found on opposite sides of the inner circle. We call this area the positive zone. Life balance and full engagement are positive but opposing characteristics. Full engagement is positive because we want people to bring their full potential to work. Yet full engagement taken too far can lead to exhaustion and become negative (see the outside circle, next to full engagement). Now let's look at the value of life balance found on the opposite side of the positive zone. If we put too much emphasis on life balance, people may withdraw from their work and give too little. Trying to create an organization where people are fully engaged and also have life balance is a complex aspiration but one without the other will likely lead us to a negative outcome.

Figure 1.1 is valuable because it shows that with the best intentions, we usually aspire to only one value in a set of opposing positive values. If we are even aware of two opposing, positive values, it is difficult to see how they can work together. Yet the ability to hold both positive notions at the same time is more likely to create a positive organization and keep us out of the negative zone. Holding two opposing ideas and creating the right balance of those ideas is a skill you can acquire. Doing so makes you more effective than the average person in your role.

The Bottom Line

I return to my friend, the young surgeon. As we concluded our conversation, he pointed out an irony. In his hospital there was a prime emphasis on both profit and growth. Yet Hospital 1 was outpacing his hospital in both areas. Hospital 1 had a more affirmative and constructive human culture as well as superior financial outcomes.[6]

He acknowledged that his observations about the two hospitals could be attributed to many other factors beyond leadership. Even so, he said, leaders matter. If people in authority have a narrow orientation to profit, technical problem solving, and linear analysis (see the bottom half of Figure 1.1) they may lack the capacity to transform a conventional or negative culture into a positive one.

What my friend was suggesting is exactly what I have seen in organizations across the globe. People, like the first CEO, have a broader mental map that gives rise to a different kind of reality. Some people value analysis, control, efficiency, and profit, but they seem to lack the generative capacity to create cultures of trust, unity, learning, and growth. Others have the opposite problem: they are quite visionary but cannot keep the system organized. A few can do both; it is as if they can live in two different worlds at the same time—the world of stability and productivity and the world of unity and change. In the next chapter we call this the ability to be bilingual.

A Diagnostic Tool

At the end of this book you will find the Positive Organization Generator. The first step in that tool is an assessment of your organization using Figure 1.1 as a guide. Applying this complex and dynamic model of thinking to your own organization, and seeing which values are high and low, should help you take a first step toward becoming bilingual. It may begin to be clear how you can live in two opposing worlds at the same time.

If you would like to make a more systematic assessment we have also developed an online version of the Positive Organization Generator on the Lift Exchange website. In this digital assessment tool you will respond to a set of questions and then receive a profile of your organization. This free online tool gives you the options to do the full version of the Positive Organization Generator, to just choose the assessment option, or to browse 100 positive practices. Feel free to share it with your unit as well. The tool is available at: http://www.liftexchange.com/generator.

Conclusion

When we talk about negative and positive organizations, we often speak in absolutes. We might say, "I work in a negative organization." This kind of language masks important truths. A human culture is complex and dynamic. It is full of human potential. Because an organization's culture is not fixed, it is always possible to move it in a more positive or negative direction. One of the biggest roadblocks to increased positivity is that many people do not understand how to make their culture more positive. For a positive organization to emerge there must be a leader who can understand the complex nature of positive and negative organizing. In the next chapter we learn how some managers do this. They become bilingual.

► **Reader Insights**

At the end of this book, you will have the opportunity to fill out the Positive Organization Generator. The first step will be to assess your unit. The second will be to create a vision for your unit. The third will be to find levers or strategies that allow your newly created vision to become a reality. You will find it helpful if you already have some. Please reflect on this chapter and then answer the following two questions.

What new characteristics would I like my unit to have a year from now?

What new ideas do I have for creating a more positive organization?

2 ▲ BECOMING BILINGUAL

Before his retirement, Alberto Weisser was the CEO of Bunge, a global food company. In his eleven years as CEO, the company grew by a factor of ten. Between the time it went public in 2001 and the time of Alberto's retirement in 2013, the stock price increased fivefold.

Alberto's story would appear to be a saga of uninterrupted success. It was not. In fact, his first year as CEO was one of the most difficult of his life.

Alberto's career was in the field of finance. He was a master of the conventional economic perspective, and that mastery carried him up the corporate ladder. He believed that an organization is a hierarchy of authority. The person at the top gives orders, and the people below follow them. If there is resistance, the CEO has to be tough. Alberto was tough; but he still sensed that he was failing. As he applied his conventional ideas of hierarchy, authority, and toughness, the organization did not move forward. Looking back, Alberto states, "I was overwhelmed and I was scared."

We tend to think of CEOs as people in positions of power who are immune to being "scared." Yet, the role of a leader is to face uncertainty and to engage unique challenges. This often means learning how to do what we do not know how to do, with the threat of failure always lurking. Scenarios like these often bring feelings of isolation and fear.

Simpleminded

Alberto followed his sentence about being scared with this one: "I was simpleminded."

19

"Simpleminded" does not mean stupid. One does not climb to the top of a corporation by being stupid. In fact, one could say that Alberto was quite brilliant. When it came to finance, he had a complex mental map that allowed him to do things others could not do. Alberto could take the most difficult financial challenges and come up with brilliant ways to move forward.

In this context, "simpleminded" means being unsophisticated about something. It means being unaware and failing to see those parts of reality that might be important to us.

Think about leaving your hometown for a far-off location. I was raised in the United States and grew up eating grilled cheese sandwiches and playing basketball. I believed my hometown was the center of the world. I remember my first trip to India. I was stunned at the poverty; exhilarated by the spirituality; stimulated by the colors; and fascinated by the economics, the politics, and the religions. I soon realized that my beliefs were a reflection of my geography. From my new experiences, I simultaneously acquired a more complex mental map and an awareness of my simplemindedness.

Alberto was "simpleminded" because he had a limited mental map when it came to organizations. He made conventional assumptions about organizations, leadership, and people. Folks who make conventional assumptions tend to believe the things listed in Table 2.1.

Where do such assumptions come from? They come from experience. They also come from thousands of studies.[1] The list in Table 2.1 reflects reality. Much of the time, people behave according to these assumptions. Alberto gained these assumptions from both his training in finance and from his daily experiences in the professional world. Unfortunately, making these kinds of assumptions nearly led him to failure. He could not create positive change by enacting his conventional or "simpleminded" assumptions.

A Transformation

Our mental maps tend to be altered by experiences that challenge our existing beliefs. One day, Alberto experienced such a jolt. Two of his senior people approached him and said: "If there is a purpose, we are not understanding it. We don't know where we're going. We're not aligned. What are we doing?"

TABLE 2.1 Assumptions in the Conventional Mental Map

Organization	The organization is a pyramid, a hierarchy of positions.
Information	Information flows to those who need to know.
Leadership	Leadership means a position of authority and directing others.
Leadership Style	Leaders are either task focused or person focused.
Motivation	Motivation follows instruction, rewards, and punishments.
Status	People get privileges based on status categories.
Change	Change is conceived at the top and is driven down the system.
People	• Pursue self-interests • Minimize personal costs • Feel fear • Prefer the status quo • Stay in their roles • Speak in politically correct ways • Fail to see opportunities • Compete for resources • Experience conflict • Become alienated • Deny feedback and fail to learn • Underperform • Personally stagnate

At one level, Alberto was shocked. They were suggesting that the short-coming was not in the organization, where Alberto had been placing the blame. They were suggesting that Alberto was not leading effectively.

A short time later, Alberto met with an equity analyst who articulated a similar view. The analyst also saw a lack of purpose and alignment. He suggested that Alberto's difficulties existed because he did not know the minds of his people. According to the equity analyst, until Alberto understood what they thought, he would not be able to align his people with the collective purpose of his company.

These two experiences were important. Alberto was beginning to recognize a painful truth that none of us likes to encounter. He needed to learn and change. He needed to transcend his existing map so that he could become more effective.

A Learning Journey

After the analyst and his own people told Alberto that the company was lacking alignment and that he didn't know the minds of his people, Alberto decided he needed to learn more about culture and how to create engagement. This was a difficult assumption because he never believed that such things mattered. To move forward, he had to transcend his own mental map. In considering the idea of creating a more positive organization, Alberto said, "I was very, very cynical about it. I never believed in any of these things."

He received help from two academics. The first was Professor Jerry Porras of Stanford University. Porras and Jim Collins had coauthored the popular book *Built to Last*.[2] Their research led to the conclusion that some companies grow and succeed because of the kind of culture they develop.

Such companies do not adopt an intense, narrow focus on profit and shareholder value. They have a core ideology and ambitious goals. The ideology or positive culture is vitalized by leadership. Leaders embody the purpose and values of these extraordinary companies. The people are inspired by the pursuit of their purpose. The cultures of these companies lead to both unity and stability. This stability, paradoxically, makes change and growth possible. The people have a positive, creative orientation as they experiment, learn, and change. The organization is a hierarchy, but it is also a thriving organism or social network, animated by continuous movement toward a collective purpose.

Alberto was impressed by these ideas but not fully convinced.[3] He continued to look for confirmation. He began to work with Daniel West of Harvard University. West had Alberto read material suggesting that when unified people are given a clear, meaningful purpose, they are able to move forward faster, persisting even when the leaders are absent.

Making Positive Change

As Alberto continued to learn, he changed. He was able to add new beliefs and assumptions to his mental map, which, in turn, allowed him to see aspects of reality that he previously did not see.

Alberto began to pay more attention to culture and to people. He developed a zeal for speed, purpose, and unity. As a result he began, among other things, to emphasize purpose, authenticity, possibility, embracing the highest good, and trusting the emergent process.

PURPOSE

Alberto told us the organization had a purpose statement: "Our purpose is to improve the food production chain."

Alberto could see our less than enthusiastic reaction and told us that he knew it did not sound "sexy." Yet improving the food production chain is one of the world's greatest challenges. Success or failure will have a huge impact on the future of humankind. Inside the company, the people understood and related to this purpose. Because they took it seriously, it was a source of inspiration.

As things began to improve, Alberto's aspirations increased. He began to expect the company to double in size every five years. To manage such growth, the company needed consistency, a set of values, and operating principles. Together, the purpose, values, and operating procedures became a meaningful framework. Once Alberto had this overall framework in place, the company started to move faster.

AUTHENTIC COMMUNICATION

Alberto told us something surprising about the communication of purpose. It was not the words that caused the company to move. It was the person saying the words, and it was how the person saying the words said them. Purpose is inseparable from integrity and authenticity. He told us that, without an authentic leader engaging in authentic behavior, words carry no power.

Many companies have statements of purpose or vision or values on a wall. Yet, often the people feel the statements are meaningless. When the chips are down, the leaders ignore their own statements. The people begin to see them as empty words—not as statements of purpose but as statements of hypocrisy—and the people become cynical.[4]

Alberto said that, at one point, one of his brightest people told him that his purpose was not a strategy. But that didn't bother Alberto: he told the man that he did not care that it was not a strategy. The key was that the approach made sense to Alberto, and when he talked about it he had passion. The people could feel that the passion was authentic. So they accepted and acted upon his words, and the company became more aligned. Alberto did not care about the academic criteria for a strategic vision. He only cared about his impact and the collective growth of the company. Alberto was real, and so were the purpose and value statements.

SEEING POSSIBILITY

While the conventional mental map makes many assumptions of constraint, Alberto aspired to greater growth. This meant orienting to possibility. Over time, his people learned to do this. In fact, they were eventually able to see and pursue possibilities he could not see. He told us: "We have six companies. We told them to double earnings every five years. The concept point was doubling in size. Their initiatives had to be inside our strategic pillars and core capabilities.

"Eight out of ten times, what they came up with worked. For the two mistakes, there was no punishment. It was okay. We were not going to lower their bonuses. We learned from the mistakes and we moved on. Sometimes they came up with ideas that I didn't believe in, and I would go to the board and say, 'Look, I have my doubts, but we have to trust them.' The board rarely voted against their proposals. Because our purpose was clear, because we had a concept point, there was cohesion. They got to decide on their own and they did marvelous things. We got into many new businesses."

Why would Alberto support an idea he did not believe in? He would support it because he was in the business of helping people see and believe in their own individual and collective possibilities. He was empowering them to see and pursue possibility. As they learned to do this, they began to help him see what was possible.

COMMON GOOD

Alberto claims that, in operating according to the aforementioned principles, "it made our people feel good about what they were doing." The feelings of the people mattered to Alberto because positive feelings are a reflection of positive energy. Alberto links their energy to the integrity of the leaders and their ability to orient to the highest good.

In one case, Alberto risked the company's relationship to a government in a very important emerging economy. He warned the leader of the country that his company would not buy their exports as long as they continued certain internal practices that were contrary to the good of the planet. When the leader changed the policy, the change was celebrated across the globe. Alberto's company, however, was silent and allowed the credit to go elsewhere; nevertheless, they knew what had happened, and the story continues to be of great consequence to them.

Alberto believes that integrity and acting on the highest good is important because it gives rise to positive energy. He says that it makes people "proud of their company. They don't leave. They have a sense of direction and energy."

EMERGENCE

Emergence means that something appears, occurs, or materializes without direction and control from the top. Alberto learned that as a leader he had to become a facilitator of development. He had to back off. He had to provide purpose and trust his people. Indeed, he had to support their ideas even when he was doubtful about them. This reliance on purpose and trust is empowering. It gives rise not only to individual initiative but also to the emergence of collective learning and creative collaboration.

As his people moved forward, Alberto noted that they sometimes failed. The failures were not punished but treated as points of learning. The key was continuing to move forward and continuing to learn. In doing this, the people were cocreating the organization. The organization was emerging in real time. It was not emerging from the mind of the person at the top. It was emerging from the interactions between all the people connected with it. This particular principle, the notion of trusting the emergent process, is far outside the conventional mental map.

It may be one of the most difficult concepts for executives to understand, accept, and act upon.

Bilingual Leadership

At the end of our interview, Alberto reflected on his learning journey. He told us that, for most of his career, he was tied to the kinds of assumptions listed in Table 2.1. He said he was particularly tied to the notion that he needed to be "the expert." He needed to have all the answers. This assumption, more than any other, accounted for his failure. He said, "If you are an imperial CEO, or if you think too much of yourself, then it doesn't work."

> Alberto then made a final point. It was seemingly insignificant and would be easy to ignore. It turns out to be quite important. Alberto told us that he does not always speak to others the way he was speaking to us. Many of the people he deals with are embedded in the conventional mental model. He has to take that into account and adjust how he communicates. He can do it because he once was where they are now. The once cynical Alberto can still speak the language of control and constraint, but he can also provide the kind of direction that empowers people and causes the organization to grow. He speaks two languages.

The process of becoming a bilingual leader is important, and the notion of learning another language is worthy of reflection. I think of a young man named James who now speaks five languages. He told me his first experience with a second language was in the seventh grade. He studied Spanish for four years. When he graduated from high school, he planned to go on a study abroad to South America, where he would put his Spanish-language skills into real-world practice. As fate would have it, he was sent to Brazil. He tells of his arrival in the São Paolo airport:

"Walking around the airport I remember that every sign, every announcement, and every person was using Portuguese. I couldn't understand anything. Even when I found someone who spoke English, it was with such a heavy accent that I was lost. It was a strange experience. I was both frustrated and fascinated at the same time. I wondered how I was ever going to learn what I needed to learn, and in the short term, how I was going to find my way through the airport and to my new home.

"Nine months later, when I finished my exchange program and was returning home, I remember going back to the São Paolo airport. I saw it with completely different eyes. I could understand everything around me without even thinking about it. It all made sense. It was this amazing transformation that you can't imagine unless you've experienced it."

When James arrived at the airport in São Paolo, it was like Alberto arriving in the office of the CEO. There was much that Alberto could not understand. Like James, Alberto underwent a learning journey and acquired new ways to feel, think, see, and act. What he acquired on his journey was a more comprehensive, positive map. If we return to Figure 1.1, we can see how he became a bilingual leader. While he was naturally strong in the bottom half of Figure 1.1, he acquired an understanding and an appreciation for many of the characteristics in the top half. Like James returning to the airport with increased ability to function, Alberto also had increased ability to function.

The Positive Mental Map

Again, the simplest definition of a positive organization is that it is a system in which the people flourish and exceed expectations. This means that the organization has a culture in which the people are engaged, collaborating, growing, and performing at an extraordinary level. The kinds of assumptions that give rise to the positive organization can be seen in Table 2.2.

The positive mental map recognizes that people are full of potential and can do things that are not imagined from the conventional mental map.

Yet, to gain the positive mental map, as Alberto did, does not mean rejecting or losing the conventional mental map: it is simply a more complex way of thinking and seeing. It is taking two ideas that appear to be in opposition and understanding how both can operate simultaneously in an organization. It is becoming bilingual in your ability to see potential as well as constraint as indicated in the above two lists. It is to see, understand, and value all the characteristics in Figure 1.1. In Table 2.3 you can see the assumptions of both maps side by side.

TABLE 2.2 Assumptions in the Positive Mental Map

Organization	The organization is a network of relationships.
Information	Information flows liberally, greatly enhancing possibility and capacity.
Leadership	Leadership means influence, regardless of authority or position.
Leadership Style	Leaders can be both task focused and person focused.
Motivation	Motivation follows purpose, inspiration, and intrinsic rewards.
Status	People are valued regardless of their status category.
Change	Change may emerge and/or be driven from anywhere within the system.
People	• Embrace the common good • Make spontaneous contributions • Feel confident • Seek growth • Overcome constraints • Expand their roles • Express their authentic voice • See and seize new opportunities • Build social networks • Nurture high-quality connections • Embrace feedback • Exceed expectations • Learn and flourish

In the next table (2.3), we see the assumptions of both maps side by side. When we embrace all the assumptions in Table 2.3, the organization can be seen as a pyramid of authority and also as a network of social relations. Information can be restricted in some cases and widely shared in others. The authority to make decisions may be invested in one person, but every person has the potential to initiate, influence, or lead. While a person may focus on task completion or on caring for people, a leader

TABLE 2.3 Becoming Bilingual: Holding Both the Conventional and the Positive Mental Maps

	Conventional Mental Map	Positive Mental Map
Organization	The organization is a pyramid, a hierarchy of positions.	The organization is a network of relationships.
Information	Information flows to those who need to know.	Information flows liberally, greatly enhancing possibility and capacity.
Leadership	Leadership means a position of authority and directing others.	Leadership means influence, regardless of authority or position.
Leadership Style	Leaders are either task focused or person focused.	Leaders can be both task focused and person focused.
Motivation	Motivation follows instruction, rewards, and punishments.	Motivation follows purpose, inspiration, and intrinsic rewards.
Status	People get privileges based on status categories.	People are valued regardless of their status category.
Change	Change is conceived at the top and is driven down the system.	Change may emerge and/or be driven from anywhere within the system.
People	• Pursue self-interests • Minimize personal costs • Feel fear • Prefer the status quo • Stay in their roles • Speak in politically correct ways • Fail to see opportunities • Compete for resources	• Embrace the common good • Make spontaneous contributions • Feel confident • Seek growth • Overcome constraints • Expand their roles • Express their authentic voice • See and seize new opportunities

(Continued)

TABLE 2.3 *(Continued)*

Conventional Mental Map	Positive Mental Map
• Experience conflict	• Build social networks
• Become alienated	• Nurture high-quality connections
• Deny feedback and fail to learn	• Embrace feedback
• Underperform	• Exceed expectations
• Personally stagnate	• Learn and flourish

of transformational influence is high on task and drives for results while also being high on people. To gain the positive mental map is to become bilingual.

Becoming bilingual broadens your worldview, making you like James on his return to the São Paolo airport: he was transformed. Recall that when James first arrived in São Paolo, he was able to navigate his way through the airport—but only with considerable difficulty; he got to his destination eventually—but not easily. Later on, having acquired the ability to speak Portuguese, he had a new capacity for navigating the terrain more effectively, faster, and with greater enjoyment. Acquiring the positive mental map works in a similar way. With the first map, you are able to manage and probably even get to where you need to go; but with both maps, you have options that will make your organization more positive and more effective. With both maps you can pursue all the positive characteristics in Figure 1.1.

Conclusion

Supervisors, managers, and executives have a mental map that guides their choices and actions. Most are led by the common, conventional map. When leaders are only familiar with this map, they are "simple-minded" like Alberto was at first. This only means that they haven't internalized assumptions that allow them to think in more complex ways about their organizations.

There is another map, the positive mental map, which offers the language of possibility. Most people don't look for or find this map unless they have experienced a crisis of some sort, which breaks down their conventional assumptions and allows them to be more open. When they do this, they begin to evolve into a more complex thinker. Acquiring this positive mental map is a lot like becoming bilingual. It is a journey, not an instant transformation. It involves taking risks, failing your way forward, and having the confidence to keep trying. Learning a new language doesn't mean forgetting your native language; rather, it adds a greater capacity to communicate and learn.

► *Reader Insights*

At the end of this book, you will have the opportunity to fill out the Positive Organization Generator. The first step will be to assess your unit. The second will be to create a vision for your unit. The third will be to find levers or strategies that allow your newly created vision to become a reality. You will find it helpful if you already have some ideas. Please reflect on this chapter and then answer the following two questions.

What new characteristics would I like my unit to have a year from now?

What new ideas do I have for creating a more positive organization?

3 ▲ CREATING A SENSE OF PURPOSE

Gerry Anderson, the CEO of Detroit-based DTE Energy, was a guest speaker at the Center for Positive Organizations. As I listened to him, I was mesmerized. His opening statement was: "Creating organizations of excellence and energy is the most real thing you can do."

Like Alberto, Gerry indicated that he did not always believe this. He had to learn to accept the idea that an organization could be excellent. As Gerry continued his story, I heard many of the same themes that Alberto had shared with me. He had experienced the same kind of hard-earned wisdom. His words were filled with insights about the nature of organizational purpose and how to use purpose to create an organization of excellence.

Gerry was trained in engineering and physics and later in finance. He took a job at McKinsey before going to work at DTE Energy. Gerry had an analytic mind, was a problem solver, and used numbers to confront and resolve "hard" issues. These tools served him well, and he became president and later the CEO of DTE Energy.

Gerry's Early Days as CEO

Gerry said that when he was lower in the hierarchy (he started at the vice presidential level) he used to see that the company's engagement scores from the Gallup global database were always in the bottom quartile. He knew that the numbers were bad, but, personally, he was indifferent. Engagement was not his concern.

When he became DTE's president, though, his perspective changed. It was a change that did not come easily. He suffered the same kind of agony that Alberto suffered as he learned his way into a new mental map.

With his promotion to president, and for the first time in his life, Gerry began to "think about the whole." He took responsibility for the engagement scores, and, as he did, he made an important discovery.

> Gerry found that DTE Energy had a problem that I believe exists in many companies. His organization had a "culture of explanation." In other words, if his managers traced a problem to the culture, the culture became an "explanation." The act of sharing the analysis would naturally excuse them from any responsibility, just as he had earlier excused himself. Culture was not seen as a tool of leadership for creating excellent organizations; it was seen as an organizational constraint. The managers "knew" cultures could not be changed.

Gerry made a decision to change things. He took the position that the people in management were the leaders of the company, and, as such, they needed to take responsibility to increase the engagement scores. Still operating from a conventional mental map, Gerry made a common assumption—the same assumption Alberto made about the need to be tough. Gerry believed that his managers needed to be pushed to accept responsibility. He began to confront them in terms of excellence and engagement. He expected everyone to know their engagement scores and to have a plan to elevate them.

To a certain degree, Gerry's strategy worked. The company's costs, for example, went down. While this might have been a cause of celebration, Gerry noticed something less promising. He was not creating a positive culture. The people were responding because of what he was imposing on them, and they were afraid. Gerry knew that fear couldn't be the basis for a sustainable, positive culture, but he didn't know what to do to create a culture without fear.

Acquiring New Beliefs

Gerry's frustration led him to wrestle with his own model of leadership. He began to question the conventional mental map and to look for some better way. He knew that, just as people have discretionary money that they can choose to spend in the economy, they have "discretionary energy" they can choose to bring to work. He wanted to access that energy.

He began to work with the idea of continuous improvement, but his efforts were disrupted by the recession of 2008. Suddenly, the company was looking at a potential loss of $175 million. With high fixed costs, the only apparent solution was to significantly reduce the workforce. Unfortunately, Gerry had spent months telling the employees that they were not "simply factors of production." To downsize would be to permanently destroy the trust he had been trying to build.

Gerry determined to do two difficult things. First, he decided not to downsize. Second, he went to the workforce with a fully authentic message. He told them downsizing would only occur as the very last alternative. He said that the company "needed the energy of the workforce as never before." He explained that he had "only a general plan" and they had to fill in the plan with their vision and initiatives. Gerry was asking the people to lead.

Gerry's message was a statement of faith in the goodness of the people and the hope that they would willingly contribute. This was new territory for Gerry, and looking back now he says that the process made him "fearful." Despite the fear, something "amazing" happened.

Each month in 2009, DTE's finance person would meet with Gerry. Each month, he would report that the company was ahead of plan. Gerry could not believe they were succeeding in such an unlikely situation and often pressed back, wondering if the financial model was broken and if the person from finance was giving Gerry the wrong numbers.

August of 2009 had all the makings of a weak month. That month, Gerry was sure the news would be bad. When the report was positive, Gerry slammed the table and said, "Your model is broken." The man delivering the report then slammed the table and replied, "My model is not broken."

Gerry points to this as a life-changing moment. Given everything he previously knew to be "real," the data could not have been true. Gerry was now confronting a positive reality that defied his conventional mental map. He had asked the people to step up, and they responded. He says thousands of efforts emerged simultaneously. Here are some examples.

The power plant control system was obsolete. Replacing the system would cost an estimated $30 million. The project team was proud when they developed a plan that got it down to $27 million. When Gerry issued his call for help, the team decided to completely reanalyze the system. They dug deeper and deeper until they discovered that they could actually replace the logic board and harvest the rest of the hardware for reuse. The cost of the project dropped from $30 million to just $3 million. When Gerry called the people into his office to thank them, they were full of goodwill and positive energy.

In the controller's office, there was much work that required outside experts. It was estimated that they were using the full time equivalents (FTEs) of 100 people. The group voluntarily took it upon themselves to eliminate those 100 FTEs. This meant creatively reframing the work and cleaning up processes. When they were done, they were fully functioning without the cost of the FTEs, and they have never turned back.

The tax group, like tax groups in most companies, was usually three years in arrears on tax audits. Being three years behind burns employee time and also requires expensive outside expertise. So the tax group initiated its own change process and now gets the task done within six months of the previous year. The 2014 audit, for example, was completed in the first half of 2015.

These kinds of spontaneous efforts took place throughout DTE Energy. Like Alberto, Gerry had to rethink what he believed. This positive data triggered a transformation. Gerry "came to see the potential in organizations."

Purpose

The positive challenges continued. In the middle of a terrible recession, Gerry watched DTE Energy flourish. He notes that "the employees took ownership of the company; they were fully engaged." They were willingly bringing their "discretionary energy" to work.

Yet, outside the company, conditions were terrible. General Motors and others went bankrupt. People all over Michigan were suffering. Given this suffering, many employees approached Gerry with a surprising question. They asked how the company could better help not just their customers but also the people in the local communities. His people genuinely wanted to contribute to the general welfare. They had a desire for the company to serve a purpose higher than profit.

Gerry reflected on this desire. He eventually called people together and shared a response. He explained that, as an energy company, they touched nearly every aspect of life in the state. If they could become the best-operated energy company, they could also focus on helping local communities. Eventually, they formulated a statement: "DTE Energy's aspiration is to be the best-operated energy company in North America and a force for growth and prosperity in the communities where we live and serve."

This statement could have fallen flat. It did not. Gerry says the idea brought meaning to their work, and it released great energy into the company.[1]

Many new projects followed. In 2010, for example, the governor invited the company to become the leader in using their purchasing power to save jobs in Michigan by buying from Michigan companies. DTE Energy was determined to undertake the challenge without undermining cost or quality. The project required finding new suppliers who typically worked in other sectors. Spending on Michigan companies climbed from $475 million to $922 million.

The positive responses also proved momentous for Gerry, furthering his process of personal transformation. He internalized a new view of reality. He moved from many of the assumptions in Table 2.1 to the assumptions in Table 2.2. He began to see potential in the people in the organization that he did not see before. He says that he learned more during this period than at any other time in his career.

And Gerry continued to learn. Among the members of the board of DTE Energy was Joe Robles of USAA. USAA is an insurance company that has a reputation for excellence. Gerry decided to go to Texas to observe Joe's company. They visited a call center, which is often a discouraging place to work. At this particular call center, however, Gerry did not find discouragement. He found people who were fully engaged in what they were doing. They had a positive work culture. They were bringing their discretionary energy to work.

What Gerry observed exceeded his expectations. He was fascinated, and he peppered Joe with questions about USAA's culture. Joe then made a momentous statement.

THE PRIMARY PURPOSE OF A LEADER IS TO
CONNECT PEOPLE TO THEIR PURPOSE.

Earlier in his career, Gerry might have resisted this notion. In the conventional mental map, the purpose of management is to solve problems, to continually return things to equilibrium, and to provide the financial incentive for people to do their jobs. But, in the positive mental map, the company is also a social network that needs to move forward collectively—learning, growing, and changing as a single unit. For this to happen, people need more than financial incentives. They also need to find meaning and purpose in their work. When they do, they give more, and the organization gets more. Gerry could now see this and was ready to pursue purpose.

Joe showed Gerry a video on how the leaders at USAA connect people to the organizational purpose. Gerry was impressed, and when he returned home, he had his people begin to work on a similar video for DTE Energy. An initial test group gave it a standing ovation. Some union members working in the plants watched it and cried. In reflecting on this moment, Gerry shared what is now a core belief.

> WHEN PEOPLE SEE THEIR WORK AS IMPORTANT,
> THEY ARE WILLING TO GIVE THEIR DISCRETIONARY
> ENERGY.

Outcomes

At DTE Energy, they continued to build on the financial turn that began in 2008. The stock price almost tripled. Engagement scores climbed into the top levels of Gallup's global database. The company has twice won the Best Place to Work Award, making it the first energy company to do so. Gerry points out that, over the years, many companies have won this award, but those companies are not "nitty-gritty utility companies with large populations of union employees."

Crucial Lessons

We can learn a lot from Alberto and Gerry. In their accounts are some crucial lessons about purpose. Here are four of them.

LESSON 1: ACCEPT THE RESPONSIBILITY FOR PURPOSE

The CEO of USAA had an excellent company and he believed that his primary responsibility was to link his people to their purpose. I believe that the primary role of every supervisor, manager, executive, and CEO is to do the same. My experience is that few believe or do this. As successful young managers, and later, even as CEOs, both Gerry and Alberto did not believe it. Alberto even derided the notion.

People at every level tell me how busy they are with "problems." They tell me there is no time for purpose. I believe that those problems are real, but I also believe the time argument is an excuse—an excuse with enough real examples to back it up so that it becomes a very "valid" way to avoid learning to operate in a new way.

I once spent a day with newly appointed three-star generals. The U.S. Army asked me to work with them because the success orientation that takes a person to the three-star level is not necessarily the same orientation that makes the person successful as a three star. The generals all agreed with the notion. They also agreed that they needed to begin operating from a more long-term, strategic perspective. They needed to better convey purpose. Yet they lived in a world of constant fires and could see no way to go beyond merely putting those fires out.

In this sense, generals were like the rest of us. They were just like Alberto and Gerry before they discovered the positive mental map. *If we are not committed to learning how to assume the strategic role of purpose finder and vision setter, we will remain in the tactical role of problem solver and information giver.* Joe Robles, the CEO of USAA, had lots of problems to solve, yet he made it his highest priority to continually connect his people to the purpose of the organization. Doing so was a choice that led to surprising, positive outcomes such as call centers filled with engaged and productive people.

Until we have a change in our mental maps, we will remain slaves to problem solving; we will fail to embrace the whole; we will continue to rationalize; we will stay busy; and we will leave purpose to others. Because most people think this way, the reader of this book has a golden opportunity.

Peter Vaill, a professor and consultant who focuses on organizational change and learning, makes four key points about higher purpose.[2] First, higher purpose must be discovered. This means it already exists and must be found. It is an unarticulated desire. A leader must have the ability to listen to every stakeholder, reflect on what is said, and conceptualize the shared and unarticulated purpose.

Second, the purpose must be acted upon. This means that the statement of purpose is real and that the leader uses purpose to govern personal and collective behavior so that integrity fills the culture.

Third, the purpose must be continually clarified. In a world of constant change, purpose tends to get lost and confusion reigns. In every action and in every conversation, the leader clarifies and creatively revivifies the purpose.

Fourth, executives avoid the work necessary to imbue an organization with purpose because it doesn't seem like real work. Executives want to complete tasks. Imbuing an organization with purpose is a requirement that never ends.

Imbuing an organization with purpose is not the work of technical problem solving. For people in the conventional mental map, it is a silly expectation. Here lies your golden opportunity.

If a prime responsibility of a leader is to create meaningful purpose, and if most authority figures reject that notion, the reader of this book may make a choice to become polished in the area of discovering and clarifying purpose.

This might be awkward at first. But practice will bring polish. Your efforts will differentiate you. You will experience greater meaning, and so will your people. You will provide the kind of leadership needed everywhere. Your career trajectory will turn upward. Learning to create meaningful purpose truly is a golden opportunity.

LESSON 2: SEE THE LINK BETWEEN PURPOSE AND LISTENING

The second lesson has to do with the purpose and listening. As Gerry indicated, there is a natural tendency for the people of the conventional mental map to "slough off" any discussion of culture and purpose. Most people cannot see the power in purpose.

At the heart of the conventional mental map are the notions of expertise, hierarchy, and control. Recall that Alberto felt his greatest flaw was his need to be the expert at the top of the hierarchy. We begin internalizing such hierarchical notions as soon as we learn to talk. The notions are reinforced in every experience. One key lesson of the positive mental map is that we do not need to be "the expert" who is in control. Indeed, the objective is to deeply listen, hear, and know the people. It is to discover the desires that are common to all and to articulate those desires in a statement that matters to all.

LESSON 3: EMBODY THE PURPOSE

In the positive mental map, people are not forced to do things. Their right to choose is always honored. They are attracted to new experiences. Research suggests that the great attractor in transformational leadership is "idealized influence." The leader represents the ideal state by modeling the ideal state. The leader transcends self-interest and continually models a genuine commitment to the collective good.[3]

As Gerry internalized the positive mental map, his desires changed. Over time, he developed a hunger for collective excellence. As a result, he engaged in new and surprising behaviors like going to his people at the start of the recession and inviting them to lead in ways that he could not. Such behaviors speak louder than words. As we discover and commit to the collective purpose, we become a living representation of that purpose.

> Leadership begins with the transcendence of the conventional mental map. Leadership is not a job, it is a calling. It means that a person is willing to go beyond convention for the good of the whole. The leader embodies the purpose. The leader reinforces the purpose in every interaction. This gives rise to positive organizing. The process of positive organizing is a process of action. When purpose moves people to action, they become more motivated. They learn and grow, and they often exceed expectations.

LESSON 4: MEET THE PEOPLE WHERE THEY ARE

You may recall Alberto's closing comment. He recognized that many people are caught in the conventional mental map. They are not bilingual. They do not understand the power of notions such as collective purpose and positive organization.

41

A person who gains the positive mental map does not lose the conventional mental map. He or she becomes bilingual and speaks to people in the language they understand.

Recall James, who went to Brazil and learned a new language. When he returned home, there were times when he would choose to use a Portuguese word over an English one. He did it because there are some words that simply don't exist in English. For example, if he wanted to talk about a special kind of Brazilian food, he felt he had to use the Portuguese term for it, leaving his family with no understanding of what he meant. It would have been easy for them to just brush it off and move on. James, however, was able to use his native English language to describe the Portuguese word to them in language they did understand. He was thus learning to navigate both worlds and help people understand things they had not yet experienced. If he had not learned to adapt, and if he had used words they did not understand, they would have begun to disregard him.

As Gerry evolved, he was able to value more of the positive characteristics in Figure 1.1. Gerry also learned that he had to use the conventional language with many of his people. In regards to the positive mental map, he notes, "They have a natural shedding mechanism for sloughing off such ideas."

Recognizing the natural tendency to slough off notions from the positive mental map is a key to effectiveness. A leader becomes more complex, starting where the people are, first getting their attention and buy-in, and then inviting them to new experiences, new ideas, and new capacities.

Conclusion

This chapter offers four lessons. First, accept the responsibility for purpose. Most authority figures do not understand how to imbue an organization with purpose. This means most organizations are highly vulnerable. Recognizing this blind spot could be a golden opportunity for you. You can use the ideas here to become a real leader.

Second, purpose derives from listening. When purpose is discovered and communicated, people can become self-empowering. They can band together and move through uncertainty without outside direction and control. They can engage in collective learning and self-organization. This is where organizational excellence originates.

Third, organizational purpose is communicated by personal commitment. Such communication involves integrity, the willingness to become what one wants to see in the organization. It involves genuine commitment to the primary role of leadership, which is to constantly and creatively clarify and revivify the purpose.

Fourth, we need to meet people where they are. Gaining the positive mental map actually promotes this process. While we are task focused, we must also be considerate, able to understand that others may be locked in the conventional mental map.

TOOLS

Quick Assessment: Purpose

We work to make money.	1 2 3 4 5 6 7 8 9 10	We work for a higher purpose.
Our work lacks meaning.	1 2 3 4 5 6 7 8 9 10	Our work has meaning.
We lack a sense of shared purpose.	1 2 3 4 5 6 7 8 9 10	We have a sense of shared purpose.
We do what we are assigned to do.	1 2 3 4 5 6 7 8 9 10	We do what we love to do.
We do not get meaningful feedback.	1 2 3 4 5 6 7 8 9 10	We get meaningful feedback.

Action Box: Imbuing an Organization with Purpose

Have your people fill out the Quick Assessment on purpose. Collect and share the results, but do not discuss them.

Ask each of your people to identify an experience when they were part of a group, team, unit, or organization that had a clear, meaningful, and shared sense of purpose. Ask them to be prepared to tell their story and share what they learned from it.

Lead a discussion based on the following questions.

- How can we best clarify our collective purpose?
- What would it mean to have a purpose that drives all decisions?
- What practices would authentically link all employees to the purpose?
- If we were successful, how would they behave when we were not present?
- What is our next step?

At the end of this book, you will have the opportunity to fill out the Positive Organization Generator. The first step will be to create a vision for your unit. The second will be to find levers or strategies that allow your newly created vision to become a reality. You will find it helpful if you already have some ideas. Please reflect on this chapter and then answer the following two questions.

What new characteristics would I like my unit to have a year from now?

What new ideas do I have for creating a more positive organization?

4 ▲ NURTURING AUTHENTIC CONVERSATIONS

Alberto and Gerry both believed the job of a CEO is to be the expert who solves problems and gets things done. They are not alone. Most people who operate from the conventional mental map believe the leader should have all of the answers. In fact, the notion of dispensing expertise permeates the world of professional organizations.

At a two-day corporate meeting, I was scheduled to be the last speaker following many recognized experts. As usual, they did a polished job of presenting important facts relevant to the audience. The first few presentations were well received. As the presentations continued throughout the event they were still excellent but the enthusiasm of the participants began to wane.

When it was finally my turn, the people were saturated and glassy-eyed. It was as if they were each holding up a sign that said, "Please, no more information, just let us go home."

Instead of pouring information on them, I started asking questions. It was the first time in the two days that there was a conversation between the person in the front of the room and the participants. I listened deeply to their comments and then, based on what I learned from them, I asked more questions.

In this genuine, learning conversation, we were equals in a mutual search for understanding. They could say or ask anything. There were no scripted answers. We were fully engaged, and we were all learning in a meaningful way.

The change in energy level was dramatic. They not only came back from the dead but also came back with enthusiasm. At the conclusion, the person in charge was particularly animated. He said the design of the two days was flawed, and that "next year the entire meeting will be a meeting of dialog and learning."

A year later, I asked some of the participants about the meeting. It turns out that dialog and learning did not take center stage. Instead, participants described two days of presentations and fact giving. The event sounded much like the one I had attended.

This story is not about how to run a corporate event, and it is not a criticism of the people running the event. This story illustrates the dominance of conventional assumptions in structuring organizational communication. Even if people understand the value of authentic dialogue, the cultural expectations are for expertise and information sharing. The notion of learning or cocreating knowledge through genuine, mutual inquiry is well outside the conventional mental map.

The conventional map reflects the political nature of organizations. Inherent in the conventional mental map is a need for self-preservation, and a fear of the vulnerability that is required in authentic dialogue. So many people hold this orientation that it is difficult to challenge it and to express an authentic voice.

My insightful friend Katie, for example, talked to me about the notion of finding an authentic voice. She explained that when we are speaking from our egos, we are not using our authentic voice.

Then Katie said, "I love the term 'find your voice.' I've worked with a couple of people in the past who have found theirs and they had amazing transformations. I never understood what authentic voice meant until I saw that. It literally means finding your real voice—not speaking as you think a professional should or with false confidence, but with your own voice. We each have one. When we do that, it shines through. It is attractive and powerful. Speaking from a place of openness demands strength and insight which results in more power and attraction."

Posturing

My friend suggests that we have an image of how a professional "should" speak. She suggests that it is often associated with "false confidence," or the need to posture and be an expert.

Once, while working with a group of nonprofit CEOs, I told a story of working with the 24 top leaders of a Fortune 500 company. The team of senior executives began by conceptualizing their desired future. We examined the gaps between their conceptualized, desired future and their own present behaviors. After that, I invited them into a situation in which they had to publicly own their shortcomings and declare what personal changes they were willing to make to bring about the collective future they claimed to desire. The exercise positively influenced the performance of the company for two years.

As I told this story, my audience of nonprofit CEOs grew quiet. I asked why they were so contemplative. One of them responded, "Because the communication process was so real. You held them accountable to their deepest moral responsibility, and we never experience that in organizations. We continually posture, but never commit in the way you were asking them to commit."

> Authentic communication is rare in organizations. Fear and political posturing are common. They both dampen engagement and learning. They hinder the emergence of the positive organization.

Posturing and Fear

Let's return to James, my bilingual friend. He went to Brazil and learned Portuguese, but since then he has learned other languages and now lives in Europe. In our conversation about becoming bilingual, he made an important observation about posturing, authenticity, and bonding.

"When I walk into any restaurant in this country, they automatically know I'm not a native. So they are gearing up to try and use English. This may make them less approachable and that will influence our interactions because we are both feeling fear. Both of us are afraid the other will judge our ability to communicate. So I try to employ humor or I ask for help, or I do something to be vulnerable. If I am speaking authentically, it helps break down the language barrier.

"If I am speaking the language to show off, which I've done, I'm simply speaking to impress the person I'm with. Whenever I do that, it's not authentic and it results in greater distance and no connection. I've learned over and over the hard way that whenever I employ my foreign language for the purpose of impressing others, it hurts communication. When I lose the front and I'm authentic and vulnerable and open to learning and trying to connect, they relax, they open up, and they usually laugh. Fear can disappear."

Posturing and Change

In an executive classroom, we were discussing the relationship between authenticity and change. A participant raised his hand. He indicated that he sits in many meetings in which a senior person introduces a proposal for change. He said, "I think to myself, this is not going to happen unless these other things also change, and they are not going to change. The speaker is not truly committed, not willing to face the realities and do the work necessary for the proposed change to really happen. So the proposal is just a dream that will eventually go away. Instead of investing in the change, I just do what is required knowing that it will eventually fade."

This comment states something that experienced people recognize and understand. Nevertheless, I found myself referring the group back to the statement time and again to address some important implications.

First, people often design and implement changes because it is their job to do so. In introducing the change, they unconsciously communicate that they are going through the required motions, but they do not have the awareness or the commitment to do all that is necessary to make the change happen. Most experienced listeners, like the man we've just quoted, are able to recognize this unspoken message.

Second, when authority figures introduce a change process and the people do not believe change is possible, they nevertheless pretend to believe. They do the things that are necessary to get by, knowing the process is not real and will eventually fade away. They engage in a ritual dance of collective pretense. Vast amounts of resources are wasted in pretending to make changes no one believes are going to happen.

Finally, as the candid executive so clearly states, "This is not going to happen unless these other things also change, and they are not going to change." Often, the authority figure, acting as an expert, does not understand the "other things" that must change and is not open to learning from those who *do know* because they are in lower roles in the hierarchy. By contrast, in the positive mental map, there is always information dissemination, but the change is driven primarily by a process of mutual learning. People authentically join with one another and cocreate the emerging future.

Authenticity and Change

"Authentic" means true, accurate, genuine, real, valid, reliable, and dependable. While it is true that when people speak with authenticity they tend to express what they are really feeling and thinking, authenticity means much more than that. The authentic person finds and expresses his or her best self. It is a self that has purpose, integrity, empathy, and openness to learning. It is a self that causes conversations and relationships to change. A woman wrote to me of her experience working in a consulting firm. Her story is an illustration of what I am proposing.

. She explained: "I helped to create a video function in my organization, and I was asked to be the director of the new team. There was a coworker who had a stronger technical expertise in video than I did who was asked to work closely with me, but was not given any title or authority. He had less time and experience with the company—and with clients—but he was a trained expert who brought skills to the group I needed and didn't possess.

"My coworker became more and more resentful of me because he knew I relied on him to provide technical knowledge in client conversations, and to lead the other video editors to a final product. I think he felt like I didn't deserve to be in charge, and that I couldn't do what I did without him.

"He would often make my life difficult by undermining what I said, by withholding information, and by complaining to the other team members. It finally got to the point where I felt like either he had to go or I had to go. I didn't want to fire him and I didn't want to quit, but I was so unhappy, I could see no other options.

"I decided to ask him to meet with me. I did a lot of soul searching and deep personal preparation. When he came in, I could tell he was defensive and upset. My natural desire was to lay out all of the reasons I was upset with him. To use my position of authority to give him "feedback." Instead, I decided to share all of the reasons I was genuinely grateful for him and his work. I then asked for feedback on what I could do better. I told him I would take notes and listen carefully.

"He was hesitant, so I told him some things I thought I could improve on that were not just surface issues. I told him I recognized that there were times I didn't allow him to lead because I was fearful that others wouldn't see me as the team leader and that they would question my role. I was terrified to be this vulnerable, but after seeing how sincere I was, he started to share. Some things he said were hard to hear, but I just listened and took notes. At the end, I restated what I had heard and committed to work on the things I needed to improve.

"By this time he had let down his guard too and was ready to reciprocate, but I told him that this meeting was just for me to hear him. I told him that after I worked on some of the things that he had given me to work on, we could get back together and talk again. I only asked that he try to be a leader to the other guys on the team and be more positive. He agreed.

"I learned something from the experience. Authenticity is not telling someone what you think you really feel about them. Authentic communication requires self-purification. It is critical that I look first at identifying my own self-deceptions and hypocrisy; otherwise nothing I say will feel authentic to my listener. It means finding and expressing your best self and doing the same for the other person. This happens when I discipline myself, when I do the work to find the things I am truly grateful for in the other person and hold myself accountable to share those things. I have to let go of fear and receive genuine feedback while also truly committing to use the feedback for self-change.

"The thing that is not easy to see in my story is that I became much more honest with myself. After that meeting, I was willing to admit how much I needed my colleague. I fully accepted a truth I had been denying. I had also been denying that I was often posturing, pretending I had capacities I did not have. I think authenticity is speaking the truth that everyone knows and no one admits so you can stop wasting time trying to prove something that isn't true and get busy helping each other do better."

This is a deeply insightful account. The woman is exhibiting a high level of positive leadership. By first changing herself, she acquired increased moral power and attracted her coworker into a new, higher quality relationship. By being authentic, she is transformational; she is changing the relationship in an unconventional way. A leader who does this consistently creates positive organizations.

The Power of the Personal

Peter Block, a well-known author and consultant on leadership in business, wrote:

> Allowing the personal to become public is the act of responsibility that initiates cultural change and reforms organizations. Our need for privacy and our fear of the personal are primary reasons why organizational change is more rhetoric than reality. Real change comes from our willingness to own our vulnerability, confess our failures, and acknowledge that many of our stories do not have a happy ending.[1]

We have noted that conventional cultures stifle authentic communication. The conventional mental map tends to frame authenticity as an illogical act. Yet, the first sentence from Block suggests that we have a "responsibility" to make the personal public. Why?

Authenticity gives rise to cultural change. It turns an organization into a more positive place. We have a responsibility to ourselves and to others to create positive organizations. In positive organizations, people begin to flourish and exceed expectations. In the end, our own highest good is the highest good of the collective. The responsibility for authenticity is the responsibility to create relationships, communities, and organizations of learning, growth, and contribution.

Research on Authenticity

Research tends to support the link between authenticity and change. Imagine a competition in which a group of business executives must make proposals to a set of judges. Alex Pentland, a professor at MIT, gathered such a group.[2] One week before their competition, he collected data on each executive. Then, without any information on what they actually presented, he predicted who would win. His predictions were 87 percent accurate!

Pentland achieved this high level of predictive accuracy by measuring how each executive sends social signals. Social signals are things like tone of voice, facial expressions, and how we physically place ourselves in relation to another. He says that humans send many kinds of signals, but there is one type that is particularly important: *honest* signals make the big difference. When people feel that communication is authentic, they open up and more fully connect to each other. Research tells us that when a leader is authentic, it is more likely that followers will shift from "fearing what they are not capable of doing, to focusing more explicitly on what they already have strengths to accomplish."[3] With such an approach, followers are able to create a "more positive possible self." That is, they are more ready to change and act in more positive ways.

Making Change Happen

Gerry Anderson said that as CEO of DTE Energy, he started out with the conventional, cultural stereotype of a good leader as someone who is decisive. The notion of a decisive leader is ego or expert based.

Both Alberto and Gerry learned that this conventional expert image has great drawbacks. Gerry says that when leaders operate from ego, as many do, all the energy "gets blocked." He says ego-driven leaders make judgments and show no curiosity. Their people are not heard, so they feel disrespected, communication becomes inauthentic, and energy does not flow.

Gerry said that there was a time when he was "all about behaving like that." He was a decisive expert. Then, he made the same change Alberto made. Gerry says, "Now I spend my time making sure that none of my people act like that. I teach them to listen. They may still have to decide, but first they listen."

A person who listens and who also decides is operating from both mental maps. By being both deliberate and decisive they are integrating two of the oppositions from the circular diagram in Figure 1.1. Here, Gerry, who has become bilingual, is teaching his people to become bilingual and, in the process, sharing his sensitivity to people and culture so that, ultimately, they will be accountable for the culture. Gerry says,

> WHEN IT COMES TO CULTURE, YOU GET JUST WHAT YOU DESERVE. IF YOU HAVE A BROKEN CULTURE, IT IS WHAT YOU DESERVE. YOU ARE NOT LEADING. YOU HAVE TO CHANGE YOUR MODEL OF LEADERSHIP. YOU HAVE TO DESERVE A DIFFERENT CULTURE.

Next, Gerry tells a story about engagement scores at DTE. They reached 96 percent for most employees, but not for the union members.

In 2012, the union engagement was at 56 percent. Gerry says, "I asked myself, what are we doing to deserve the union behaviors we have?"

Gerry went to a meeting with union leaders. The purpose of the meeting was to announce that the company had reached a new record on safety. When the announcement was made, one union leader immediately began to complain about an unrelated point of dissatisfaction. Another union member immediately followed with a similar complaint.

Gerry was stunned. He was expecting them to celebrate. One of the primary reasons unions were formed in the first place was to increase safety. Yet, any sense of celebration was overshadowed by complaints.

Gerry was supposed to give a talk at the event but chose instead to take an unconventional route. He opened "a real conversation about what was really going on."

Gerry shared how he felt, he asked genuine questions, and he listened. He modeled the behavior described in this chapter, and the union members responded. In the conversation, a consensus emerged. Eventually, there was agreement to focus on safety, engagement, and training. What was the outcome?

"In 2012, we set a goal to get the union to the top quartile (of engagement) by 2016. We reached it in 2014. It only took a year and a half. The engagement scores for the union climbed to 80 percent."

Gerry is making an extraordinary statement. It violates what we supposedly "know" about management-union relationships. We "know" that unions do not turn positive. We "know" that authentic conversations are not a leadership tool that works with unions. But, as Gerry's success shows us, our conventional assumptions can keep us from fully appreciating the power of authenticity.

Nurturing Authenticity

In a workshop in which we were exploring the role of personal integrity and moral power, I shared an account of the Indian independence leader Mohandas Gandhi facing a challenge. He was trying to stop a civil war. His unusual strategy was to change himself, so he committed to living with increased integrity or moral power.

Pondering the courage of Gandhi and his commitment to nonviolence seemed to inspire the group. A woman raised her hand and spontaneously volunteered, "My grandmother used to talk about turning fear into faith. I thought I understood that, I thought that was just about God and her own personal life. But now I see something I never saw before. It is also about me at work. I can turn my fear into the faith to make things better. I can help others do the same."

The personal reference was surprising. Admitting that she had fears seemed even more surprising. Still, everyone could identify with her fears. Her declaration that she could change held everyone's attention. There was a meaningful silence.

Then a lot of hands shot up. Each person said something equally personal. In fact, the entire discussion was honest and positive.

A person with the courage to be authentic raised her hand. She said, "I sometimes become externally directed instead of internally directed. I do something I should not do because I'm afraid. Then I feel sick inside."

There was another silence, but this time no one raised their hand. All the participants looked to me for some kind of direction. Instead of speaking from my head, I chose to be as authentic and as vulnerable as she had become. I said, "Yes, I know that feeling. Because I have high standards for myself, and because I often behave in ways that fall below my standards, I get that sick feeling inside, too."

This public confession of my own concerns about integrity was surprising, but again everyone could relate. The truth is that we all fall short of our own standards at times. But our duplicity is usually not discussable.

I went on. "Because I do not want to face the pain associated with my own failure of integrity, I try to deny and rationalize what I have done, but the sick feeling does not go away until I clarify my purpose and my values and make a change in my life's trajectory."

As I uttered that sentence, I felt fully connected to that group; I believe they were fully connected to me, as well. The room was full of trust. The room was also full of learning. The learning was unfolding at both the individual and collective levels. At that moment, the people were respectful, collaborative, and able to constructively build off each other's ideas. The climate was authentic and positive.

With the increased authenticity and positivity, we next turned to the question of the organization's culture. We were able to talk about issues that normally cannot be discussed, and we made significant progress in specifying the desired culture and how the participants could create it.

Speaking Truth to Power

I was interviewing a CEO. He was a financially focused and hard-driving Wall Street executive. He told a story of a young employee who made a mistake and lost some money for the company. As I listened to the story, I knew I was talking to a man who had become bilingual. Here is why.

The young man who made the mistake visited the CEO and began to tell his story. The CEO sat quietly, listened to every word, asked if there was anything else. When the young man was clearly finished, the CEO thanked him for the visit, reassured him, and then sent him on his way. After telling the story, the CEO asked a question, "Do you think that was my instinctual response?"

He said his natural reaction would have been to become irate and to jump all over someone who had made such a mistake. Why did he not follow his natural inclination? Over time, this CEO has learned something counterintuitive: Following his natural instincts would only get him the short-term reward of exercising his authority and venting his frustrations.

While it might appear that a punitive response would have corrected the problem, he would, in fact, have only created a much bigger one. In attacking the employee, he would have created a conventional, closed culture in which truth will not speak to power. It would also become likely that the employees would not relate to each other in authentic ways. In a conventional, closed culture, people live in fear. Some executives actually believe this is a good thing. They want their people to be afraid. It increases the executive sense of control. Yet, people who live in fear tend to underperform. The conventional, fear-based logic is a logic in which everyone loses.

The evolved CEO also understands another point. A senior executive never has a conversation with one person. The entire organization is continually heeding the signals emanating not only from the words of the senior person but also from his or her behavior.

Every conversation is a building block of the organizational culture. A conversation with one is a conversation with all. Because this particular CEO has learned to transcend his natural orientation, he regulates his own behavior and chooses to enact the assumptions typical of a positive mental map.

In most organizations, that does not happen, and both truth and power decay. In managing your own unit, you may be wise to evaluate the extent to which you create a culture that lets power speak to you. Why?

> In a positive culture, truth speaks to power and power listens and changes. In such an organization, the people can more effectively cocreate the emerging future. Through authentic dialog, people in lower positions also begin to feel safe and able to look at shortcomings. Authenticity allows people at all levels to open to all of reality. When everyone is open, everyone can join in learning how to change.

When people live in authentic communication, they tend to bond. They are more willing to pursue the collective good. As they do, the collective intelligence intensifies and everyone begins learning, growing, and performing at a higher level. The organization then becomes a positive organization, and the people feel the activity is worthy of still more human investment. The following exercises may help your people to understand and pursue greater authenticity at work.

Conclusion

The conventional organization is dominated by assumptions of expertise flowing down the hierarchy. Even when people become aware of the dysfunctions of this perspective, they continue to employ it because they can't imagine operating in any other way. The result is posturing rather than authenticity.

Research confirms that people recognize posturing and authenticity and respond to both in kind. Authentic people turn themselves into invitations to authenticity. Their direct reports become authentic, and so does their culture. Authentic communication makes it possible to embrace reality and possibility with confidence.

Some leaders come to discover that authentic conversations give rise to engagement, learning, and change. In such an organization people pursue the common good and learn in real time. The culture turns positive, and everyone grows. Authentic leadership begins with clarity of purpose and values. As the leader acts with increasing integrity, the capacity to nurture a positive culture increases.

TOOLS

Quick Assessment: Authenticity

We only say what is politically correct.	1 2 3 4 5 6 7 8 9 10	We say what we really feel.
We do not treat each other with respect.	1 2 3 4 5 6 7 8 9 10	We treat each other with respect.
We avoid dealing with difficult issues.	1 2 3 4 5 6 7 8 9 10	We constructively confront one another.
We shoot down each other's ideas.	1 2 3 4 5 6 7 8 9 10	We build off each other's ideas.
We punish mistakes.	1 2 3 4 5 6 7 8 9 10	We learn without blame.

► **Action Box: Authenticity**

Have your people consider the Quick Assessment on authenticity. Collect and share the results, but do not discuss them.

Have people read the following statement and answer the related questions.

Statement

"Authenticity appeals to me. I want to be authentic, but it is not possible. In my organization I would be punished and eventually pushed out. I cannot be authentic at work."

Analysis

- What is your first reaction to this statement?
- Is it proactive or reactive?
- Which mental map does this represent?
- How many people think like this?
- To what kind of behavior does this assumption lead?
- What role does leadership play in causing people to come to such a perspective?
- Formulate a proactive strategy for turning any organization authentic.

In your meeting, ask the people to break into pairs and formulate strategies for making the organization more authentic. Have each pair report. Then create a common strategy for creating a culture of increased authenticity.

► **Reader Insights**

At the end of this book, you will have the opportunity to fill out the Positive Organization Generator. The first step will be to assess your unit. The second will be to create a vision for your unit. The third will be to find levers or strategies that allow your newly created vision to become a reality. You will find it helpful if you already have some ideas. Please reflect on this chapter and then answer the following two questions.

What new characteristics would I like my unit to have a year from now?

What new ideas do I have for creating a more positive organization?

5 ▲ SEEING POSSIBILITY

Once a finance officer told me, "My job is supposed to be negative. I have to look for what is wrong. My job is to say 'no.' I expect people to hate me. I do not expect to be friends with the people who work for me, either. I find my friendships outside of work."

The image is dismal but prevalent. I have talked to hundreds of professionals—just like the woman I've quoted—who make similar assumptions. They accept their fate because they believe that what they experience is a reflection of the reality of business and of organizational life. They live in the reality of constraint; an invitation to a better future is met with great suspicion.

Beneath that suspicion, though, there is often is a hidden orientation to possibility, a hope that things might be better. I was impressed by the authenticity of this seemingly "negative" woman. She made her statement after asking me what my keynote address was on. I indicated that the topic was creating positive organizations. It was then that she expressed her negative assumptions. The interesting thing, however, is what happened after the keynote. She cared enough to attend the follow-up workshop. This meant, despite what she had said, that there was a small germ of belief in possibility and a small spark of hope—enough to motivate her to be present.

During the next hour, we reviewed some concepts, and then I exposed her and the other workshop attendees to the Positive Organization Generator. The tool contains 100 unusual, positive practices used by real companies. These concrete practices tend to capture the interest of even skeptical people. I ask participants to examine the practices with an eye toward customizing them to their own needs.

At the end, I challenged several of the participants to convince me that they had at least three positive practices they were ready to go home and try. I made it a point to include the "negative" woman, and she shared the three practices she wanted to try. She was going to go home to make a first attempt at creating a more positive organization. Given her initial statement, this fact genuinely excited me.

The Power of Encountering Excellence

A few days later, I visited a CEO and three of his key executives. For a year, the CEO had been advocating the creation of a positive organization. The key people, holders of the conventional mental map, could not grasp his message. After months of talking, the CEO took another path. He and his leadership team spent two days visiting a company called Zingerman's, a nationally recognized business in Ann Arbor, Michigan. Zingerman's is considered the epitome of a positive organization.

The company was founded in 1982 by Ari Weinzweig and Paul Saginaw. They started with a deli and a passion for producing great food. They organized around a genuine commitment to the community, to customers, and to employees, and they created intense commitment at all three levels. In a relatively short time, Zingerman's became recognized as one of the best small businesses in the United States. Based on their success, outsiders encouraged them to franchise the deli. Instead, they invented a new business model. Seeking to preserve their purpose, vision, and values, they began to start new but related businesses in the Ann Arbor area. Today, they have the deli, a bake house, a creamery, a training company, a mail-order business, and other kinds of restaurants. In terms of leadership, they go to extraordinary lengths to make a difference; their stories of employee, customer, and community engagement are legendary. The people at Zingerman's bring their discretionary energy to work.[1] They love what they are doing.

When the CEO and the three executives visited Zingerman's, the impact was as expected. By the time they reached the Center for Positive Organizations, they were "on fire." They were brimming with ideas about how they were going to go back and implement new practices. The ideas were inspired by what they observed at Zingerman's. There are lessons here.

> First, people caught in the conventional mental map may be full of fear or doubt, but, despite what they believe, say, or do, most have a desire for a better future. Beneath their conventional fears is a hunger for a better life. This means there is a potential in organizations that many fail to see. The leader's task is to see the latent potential, to ignite the spark, and to build belief in the reality of possibility.

Second, telling is less persuasive than seeing and doing. The CEO was unable to "talk" his executives into understanding and pursuing the creation of a positive organization. His people were locked into the conventional mental map. Given their assumptions of reality, what he was calling for did not make sense. It was a foolhardy dream.

Yet, by briefly visiting a positive organization, their beliefs were rapidly altered. Like the finance officer who was exposed to the practices in the Positive Organization Generator, the CEO found a spark of belief, and it quickly turned into a flame of desire. The people could suddenly see a way to make a difference, and they were anxious to try.

Over the years, I have tried to train myself to constantly look for patterns of excellence and then find ways to use them to penetrate the conventional mental map. Here is an illustration of how the strategy can work.

Two Invitations to Constraint

I was slated to visit the Republic of Georgia in Eastern Europe. I had been asked by my son-in-law, who was the cultural attaché at the U.S. Embassy, to address a group of 250 people at the Bank of Georgia. Separately, I was also asked to help with a cultural challenge in a work section at the embassy.

At the bank, half of the 250 members of the audience did not speak English. They would have headphones for simultaneous translation. I mentioned my interest in engaging the group in a dialog. The sponsors explained that, in past sessions, the audience had always been shy. It was part of Georgian culture.

In the embassy work section that I was asked to help, there was a large group of Georgians who had worked there for years. They were managed by Americans who typically served for only two to three years at a time. The Georgians were described by the Americans as being resistant to change. The Americans, on the other hand, were described by the Georgians as having a tendency to come in with a change agenda, as generally not listening to the Georgians, and as rarely being able to get them to talk in the first place. Since external resources were shrinking and the workload was increasing, there was a need for the Americans and Georgians to collaborate more fully, but such collaboration was prevented by the existing organizational culture.

They patiently explained that American approaches to engagement would not work in their country. I should simply plan to present information. I was strongly advised not to anticipate meaningful participation of any kind.

These were two invitations to live in the conventional mental map. I have had many such invitations. The pattern is usually the same. The sponsors or authority figures patiently explain their "unique culture" and the constraints embedded in the culture. Typically, the constraint is that the lower-level participants in the culture have spent their lives passively listening to teachers, bosses, and other experts. When asked for their opinions, which isn't often, they never speak up.

The statement made by the Georgians about my "American" approach makes me smile. Everywhere I go in the United States, I run into people who want me simply to present information. They also patiently explain why in their supposedly "unique" culture the people do not necessarily speak openly. Often, the explanation is that an authority figure will be in the room, and it will not be possible for people to speak up. After all, the organization is a political system.

While nationality does play a role, the real issue is not the geography of the planet but the geography of the mind. People in organizations across the planet live in fear. Staff who plan events tend to take the safe route. They design events to be processes of information dissemination, and their people are thus further trained to be passive recipients. No other alternative can even be imagined, for it would be outside the conventional mental map.

The misconception across the planet is that positive organizations cannot be created in a given context. What we believe determines what we can imagine. What we believe determines the reality we will continually bring into existence by our behavior. To turn an organization positive, we have to increase consciousness. Exposing people to a surprisingly positive context does this. It opens them to the positive mental map.

Finding Positive Deviation

During my first few days in Georgia, my daughter and son-in-law took me to see some of the more prominent historic places. One was a monastery. We took a brief tour and left. I did not think that my visit there was much different than visits to other such places. Yet, in the early hours of the next morning, when I pondered the previous day and wrote in my gratitude journal, I began to see things I did not fully appreciate when they actually happened. Here is what I wrote:

> David the Builder: Yesterday we visited a monastery. At the entrance of the monastery is the grave of David the Builder. He is considered the greatest king of Georgia. He brought order to a troubled land, centralized state administration, reformed the army and drove out the Seljuk Turks, reunited splintered regions, resettled devastated regions, liberated much of Eastern Georgia, promoted Christianity, and continued to have major military successes. After a thousand years, the people are still proud of him. He asked that, when he died, he be buried in the entrance of the monastery so that every entering person would have to step on his grave.
>
> Hundreds of years after his death, I did the will of this visionary king. Engaging in the unconventional act of standing on the grave of a great king, I had to consider his life and his message. I felt admiration for the visionary ability of David the Builder. He was able to alter my behavior and teach me hundreds of years after his death.

As I finished writing in my journal, I had a realization that would not have come if I had not taken the time to write. Reflecting on the notion of possibility, my attention was returned to David the Builder. He was considered the epitome of excellence in Georgian leadership history. I knew what I needed to do to help the Georgians leave their conventional map behind.

Possibility

After being introduced to the audience of 250 people, I stood and asked the Georgian audience if, in their culture, it was common to help strangers. They nodded their heads. I told them I needed help. I needed them to teach me about their greatest king.

I asked them to talk to the person sitting next to them and see if they agreed on the three most important things I should know about David the Builder. They had 90 seconds to decide, and then I would ask them to teach me. The room went dead quiet. Then, after about five seconds, the room exploded with animated discussions.

When I regained their attention, they enthusiastically taught me about the greatness of David the Builder. I then connected everything we covered back to what they taught me about the King. They remained very responsive, and we were able to engage in a level of learning the sponsors later said they had not believed possible.

> In the past, the audience had always been reticent, reserved, and non-responsive. Those assumptions were now violated. The audience became more animated and more positive. The exposure to their own, Georgian excellence—even through events that occurred a thousand years before—opened their minds. They were seeing possibility. Conventional barriers were falling.

Seeing Possibility at the Embassy

The next day, I went to work with the group at the embassy. There were 6 American managers and 16 Georgian supervisors. Everyone looked uneasy.

I asked all the Georgians to stand up and gather at the far end of the room. They were shocked, but they complied. I told them that in a few minutes I wanted them to teach the Americans about the greatness of Georgian leadership. I particularly wanted them to teach the Americans about David the Builder. So, in two minutes, I would call on each of them to give me one fact about David the Builder. They had two minutes to huddle, share facts, and make sure every person had a unique fact. After a few seconds, the group began to buzz.

As with the previous group, the Georgians in the embassy shared with enthusiasm. Their eyes lit with pride as they told of their own historical greatness.

I then asked them to compare their work section at the embassy with the condition of Georgia when David became king. They told of the great challenges he faced and how he overcame them. I listened closely and then asked if we were in a similar, dire time, and what would happen to the work section if budgets continued to shrink and if the work section did not benefit from great leadership. They told me that bad things were likely to transpire, including the loss of jobs. I told them that today was their chance to bring Georgian leadership to a difficult situation.

Each of the American managers was asked to go to a different table. I asked the Georgian supervisors to select any table except the one that included their boss. I then gave each group of Americans and Georgians a sheet of paper and asked them to do a strategic analysis of the past, present, and future of the work section. By the end of the analysis, everyone agreed that resources were shrinking, that workload was increasing, and that increased collaboration was crucial.

Each group was given a tool for culture analysis and asked to describe their current culture, as well as the culture they needed to prosper in the future. They came to an impressive consensus.

Finally, each person was asked to outline a "David the Builder Memo" to their boss. In the first half of the memo, they were asked to indicate three investments they were willing to make in the cultural change process. The investments would include behaviors they had never before engaged in, behaviors consistent with the new culture, behaviors that they would actually be excited to try. The second half of the memo was to include three invitations to their boss. The invitations should be requests regarding how they would like their boss to behave so as to bring about the desired culture.

They then read their individual outlines aloud at each table. The other people at the table provided coaching on how each memo could be improved. At the end, we all agreed that the memos would be sent by the end of the next workday and that all managers would share the information with their higher level bosses and get back to the group with a response within a few days.

In the course of a few hours, Americans saw behavior in their Georgian coworkers that was completely new. Georgians saw behavior in the Americans they had never seen before. These new behaviors were signals of possibility. The people who came into the room looking uneasy left the room looking hopeful. They had shifted from a focus on constraint to a focus on possibility. They were about to try new behaviors. They were beginning to believe that they could build a more positive organization.

We had opened the window of change. How much change would follow would be determined by their supervisors and their ability to be leaders. Some supervisors would unconsciously crush the process. Others would keep it alive. In the end the ability to lead culture change matters a great deal.

Challenging Constraint

What happened in these two Georgian experiences? I was in a country I had never before visited. I did not understand their language, and I had been warned that in the Georgian culture, the people would not respond to engagement techniques.

I did not accept these assumptions. I believed that the people in both settings had a desire to live in a better condition. The challenge was to ignite the desire. The strategy was to violate the expectations of their conventional mental maps. Since excellence is not conventional, introducing it is a positive distortion. Such positive variance captures attention and opens the mind. As I continued to call them to excellence, I was nurturing the belief and sparking the hope that already existed, even though no one could see it.

Belief in Our Own Excellence

A reader who is wedded to the conventional mental map may be thinking right now: "Quinn may be able to do things like this, but I cannot. He is describing a very high level of skill that I do not have."

Such a response is natural. When we introduce change in an organization, our people often experience similar feelings of helplessness. Yet, I think there is considerable hope for the reader who responds in this fashion.

I was talking to a man who had learned the positive mental map and was very committed to it. In the meeting, the discussion shifted to the notion of constraint. The man interrupted and said: "What I have learned is that I do occasionally have moments of greatness and I am exposed to a better me, actually to my best self. When I bring forth this best self, I tend to be excellent. Aware of this, I can now reflect on my moments of greatness and ask how to be excellent more often. I can coach myself to be proactive about it. I can focus on how to be excellent today."[2]

> Since excellence is almost always an episodic rather than a permanent condition, most people correctly believe that they are not excellent. Because of this correct assumption, they make a second, incorrect assumption. They choose to incorrectly believe they cannot be consistently excellent. In the same fashion, they conclude that their organization could never be excellent.

This often locks them into the conventional mental map. The reality of constraint blinds them to the reality of possibility. Because they lack faith in themselves, they slough off the image or possibility of being excellent, personally or collectively.

The fear of failure then becomes a self-fulfilling prophecy. The person who gives up continues to experience failure to become excellent, and the fear of failure only grows stronger. Reflecting on our own moments of greatness is important because it opens us to our own possibility and gives us the courage to imagine and pursue the excellence that is waiting to be realized.

> If we are willing to entertain the possibility of our own growth, we can experience episodes of excellence. As we recognize the excellence in ourselves, we can begin to look for the excellence in others. We can become expert at locating it, and we can use it to spark hope and stimulate people to new actions and new learning. In the process, we invite them to discover the positive mental map.

You may not do it the way I did it in Georgia. You may not do it the way the CEO did it when he took people to Zingerman's. If, however, you are growing and feeling the unfolding of your own potential, you will see the potential in others; you can then find your own way to expose them to excellence so as to nurture their belief and spark their hope. It is something you learn to do in your own unique way.

71

Conclusion

Many people, like the financial officer who felt it was her job to be negative, make assumptions of constraint. The truth is that many people actually desire a better future, but they don't believe it is possible. Leaders can talk to their people about creating a positive organization, but nothing happens until they are exposed to excellence. Seeing excellence accomplishes something that "telling" cannot accomplish. It challenges the conventional mental map and invites them to discover their way into the positive mental map.[3]

When we move to the positive mental map, we accept the reality of constraint (to honestly assess and get grounded), while we pursue the reality of possibility (to move forward and grow). As leaders, we can learn to continually search for excellence, and we can use it to change the culture. In Georgia, I walked into two unfamiliar contexts believing—despite tales to the contrary—that Georgians wanted to engage, just like the people in every other country.

People everywhere need only to have someone link them to their own excellence so that they can see the possibilities, and then support them in exploring the present. In Georgia, I believed that together we could go places they had never been. I invited them to excellence, and they chose to join me. We had new experiences, and the conventional culture began to change. As we shifted to possibility, we initiated the emergence of a more positive culture.

TOOLS

Quick Assessment: Possibility

We focus on constraints.	1 2 3 4 5 6 7 8 9 10	We focus on possibilities.
We are pessimistic.	1 2 3 4 5 6 7 8 9 10	We are optimistic.
We are reactive.	1 2 3 4 5 6 7 8 9 10	We are proactive.
We seek to solve problems.	1 2 3 4 5 6 7 8 9 10	We seek to spread excellence.
We are trapped in our own past.	1 2 3 4 5 6 7 8 9 10	We are creating a new future.

► *Action Box: Seeing Possibility*

Have your people fill out the Quick Assessment on possibility. Collect and share the results, but do not discuss them.

Next, have your people complete the following exercise. Have them share their responses, and then discuss some common strategies they can use to orient their people to possibility.

Identify a person, group, unit, or organization that you know well and that is excellent. Answer the following questions.

- Are there moments of greatness in the history of any of the individual people?
- Are there moments of greatness in the history of the unit?
- Are there any individuals who are currently performing beyond expectations?
- Are there any subgroups currently performing beyond expectations?
- Are there any individuals or organizations outside the unit performing beyond expectations?

Based on your answers to these questions, specify at least three ways to expose your people to excellence. List your strategies.

Discuss the answers and formulate a strategy for your overall organization.

At the end of this book, you will have the opportunity to fill out the Positive Organization Generator. The first step will be to assess your unit. The second will be to create a vision for your unit. The third will be to find levers or strategies that allow your newly created vision to become a reality. You will find it helpful if you already have some ideas. Please reflect on this chapter and then answer the following two questions.

What new characteristics would I like my unit to have a year from now?

What new ideas do I have for creating a more positive organization?

6 ▲ EMBRACING THE COMMON GOOD

"Did you know that organizations are political?"

When this question is posed to a class of executives, the typical response is a low laugh. The laugh signifies that the answer is so obvious, it borders on being silly. "Everyone knows that organizations are political; if you did not know this, you would not survive."

There is a follow-on question. "Have you ever had a boss who chose his or her personal good over the collective good?"

Usually, every hand goes up. I then ask, "How did you react when the boss made the self-interested decision?"

The most typical answer is, "I lost respect, I stopped caring, and I withdrew."

An Elusive Concept

The conventional mental map assumes that people are self-interested. The positive mental map assumes that people can be enticed to pursue the collective interest. When the latter assumption is realized, the organization turns positive. My desire is to move people from the natural pursuit of self-interest to the unnatural pursuit of the collective good. Given this desire, I teach an elusive concept: an organization is not only a political system but also a moral system.

The word "moral" means ethical, principled, honorable, honest, or good. In organizations, the word can make people uncomfortable. It seems like a term better suited to a church gathering than to a boardroom meeting. After all, the essence of business is competition, the survival of the fittest.

I was listening to a talk by a marriage counselor. The speaker described the positive feelings that two people tend to have when they first marry. Then he described emergent patterns of resentment, disengagement, and isolation. He described people living together in cold civility while being emotionally alienated. He then spoke of divorce, explaining that most of the failed marriages could have been saved if the people had known how to relate to each other more effectively.

I was struck by how perfectly this description fits organizations. Over time, people tend to become resentful, disengaged, and isolated. Since no one knows what to do about it, the conflict lingers beneath the surface, and people live in cold civility. In such a context, everyone tends to seek their own self-interest.

When the people are oriented to a higher good, they tend to unify, transcend self-interest, and sacrifice for the whole. The organization becomes healthier. What we will see in this chapter is that it is very difficult to repair and maintain the moral system of an organization. I am reminded of a great insight from Henry David Thoreau's 1849 essay, *Civil Disobedience*:

"Action from principle, the perception and the performance of right, changes things and relations; it is essentially revolutionary, and does not consist wholly with anything that was. It not only divides states and churches, it divides families; aye, it divides the individual, separating the diabolical in him from the divine."[1]

Here are some key points:

- The pursuit of principle is change.
- It is a break from the past. It is a new, even revolutionary behavior that threatens the collective equilibrium or comfort zone.
- It is a source of conflict that divides people in families, groups, and organizations.
- It even divides the individual, separating the best, growing self from the worst, stagnant self.

To understand them, we turn to an illustration.

Moral Power and Social Change

42 is the name of a 2013 film about the life of the legendary baseball player Jackie Robinson. In 1946, Branch Rickey, general manager of the

Brooklyn Dodgers, recruited Robinson as the first black player in major league baseball. In one of the film's opening scenes, Rickey spells out the abusive behavior that Robinson will face and wants to know if Robinson will be able to handle it. Confused, Robinson asks if Rickey wants a man with enough courage to fight, but Rickey shakes his head and responds that he wants a man with enough courage *not* to fight.

It is clear from the beginning that Rickey has a profound understanding of what is going to transpire. He understands that if he invites Robinson to play for his team, a deep cultural change will need to take place within the team, in baseball, and in society. He also recognizes that making that change will require a kind of power that trumps the political power at the heart of the conventional mental map. It will require moral power.

Power means influence. Moral power is the influence that comes when we choose to live from principle rather than political pressures. Moral power is particularly visible when a person pursues a selfless, ideal cause—a cause that reflects the common good.[2]

Deep Change

Another way to interpret what Thoreau said is to embrace the notion of "deep change." When a person pursues the collective good in a politically driven context, that person is modeling unconventional behavior. This positive deviation attracts attention and requires people to think and to make choices of their own. In the process of observing new options, thinking, and choosing, some people experience "deep change"—an alteration in their basic mental map. Consider two illustrations from *42*.

Initially, the Dodgers players—like most everyone else—were against Robinson. The culture was one of self-interest, and players didn't want to lose their position, their playing time, or their comforts. Over time, they watched Robinson absorb brutal abuse. At one point, an opposing manager stood outside the dugout and poured continuous hateful statements on Robinson. Robinson's refusal to respond or defend himself sparks a change in the Dodger players. One player who was not particularly welcoming to Robinson when they first met finally stands up, walks across the field, and threatens to attack the opposing manager if he says another word.

Later Branch Rickey wisely notes that the opposing manager was actually helping the cause. He explained that when someone is abusive like the opposing manager, and the recipient does not respond, people feel sympathy for that person. He says sympathy means "to suffer with." The opposing manager's abuse, coupled with Robinson's self-discipline, caused the Dodger players (as well as the fans) to feel for and suffer with him.

> WHEN WE SUFFER WITH SOMEONE, THE PERSON IS NO LONGER AN OBJECT THAT WE REJECT BECAUSE HE OR SHE IS DIFFERENT; THE PERSON BECOMES A FULLY HUMAN BEING FOR WHOM WE HAVE COMPASSION BECAUSE WE SEE THE GOODNESS IN THE PERSON.

The manager's natural bigotry and hateful behavior was important to the change process. The attack allowed Robinson to make a courageous choice. Because he was committed to a higher purpose, he did not engage in fight or flight. He chose to suffer for the purpose that was higher than himself. This kind of self-sacrifice is principled or moral behavior, and it is "a break from the past."

Robinson was not acting according to conventional expectations. His was a "new" or "revolutionary" kind of behavior. Such moral behavior captures attention and requires people to examine their own values and make a decision. When people have to choose between conventional norms and living their deepest values, there is a likelihood of conflict both within and between individuals.

The conflict "divides" groups. It also "divides" the individual, who must choose between the birth of a new self or the protection of the conventional self.

As Robinson pursued the higher good, he attracted people to the collective good. His suffering brought sympathy, and the new feelings led to new perceptions. The differentiation on the team ("us" versus "him") was transformed into an integration ("we, the team" versus "them, the outside persecutors").

A new and shared mental map was emerging among the increasingly unified players. They were pursuing the common good. This was a cultural change on the Dodger team. It would eventually become a cultural change outside the team.

In another scene from the film, the Dodgers are about to play in Cincinnati. Pee Wee Reese, star shortstop for the Dodgers, is from nearby

Kentucky. Reese enters the office of Branch Rickey with a sense of indignation. He shows Rickey a letter. Someone in Kentucky has called Reese a carpetbagger and offers a threat. Reese is incensed, but Rickey is unimpressed by the letter. He pulls out several thick files of hate mail, filled with vicious threats, that had been sent to Robinson. Reese is stunned by what he reads and begins to further understand what it must feel like to be Jackie Robinson.

The next scene is in the ballpark in Cincinnati. A father and young son are talking. The son is a Reese fan and says he hopes Reese performs well. The father responds tenderly and tells a story of when he was a boy and watched his favorite player do well. At that moment, the Dodgers take the field, and the tender father suddenly yells malicious and discriminatory insults at Robinson. The boy watches with curiosity . . . and then does the same.

This single scene offers two jolting moments. First, we discover that a man capable of being a tender father can also be a vicious racist. Second, we watch a relatively innocent boy observe the father he loves and then adopt his hateful behavior. It is one small illustration of the mix of nobility and frailty in all of us, and of the fact that we all live in fear when our conventional, cultural assumptions are threatened.

As the scene continues, the majority of the fans vilify Robinson. Pee Wee Reese observes this, and then does something shocking. He makes a choice to live from principle, to pursue the higher good. He runs over to Robinson, and puts his arm around him. Robinson asks Reese what he is doing. Reese gives a profoundly important answer, "I want these people to see who I really am."

Reese has had his basic assumptions challenged. In the process, he has to clarify his values and determine if he is going to live comfortably by convention or courageously by conscience. To live by conscience and by principle is to break from his own social past and to anger many of the people in his social network. However, it is also a chance to release his best emerging self, to divide it from the conventional self.

This new, courageous self is more virtuous and more self-empowering. It is a self he can better love. When we have a self we can love, strangely enough, ego needs decline. We become more oriented to the higher good and to the highest common good. We more readily see the potential in others, and we become more empowering to the community in which we operate. We are more likely to look for the common good and invite them to embrace it.

Eco-Perspective

While the person who lives from the conventional mental map is likely to be skeptical about the ability to transcend self-interest, research suggests that it does happen. The desire to transcend self-interest and to make a positive difference in the lives of others is called "prosocial motivation."[3]

Research indicates that people who experience prosocial motivation are more likely to take initiative, assist others, persist in meaningful tasks, and be open to negative feedback.[4]

The research also shows that people like Reese, who pursue the common good, are more likely to motivate others, stimulate them to new ideas, and inspire their creativity. These facts suggest that prosocial people orient to the positive mental model. They shift from a focus on the "ego-system" to a focus on something called the "eco-system."

The term "eco-system" in this context comes from the work of Otto Scharmer and Katrin Kaufer.[5] They see the "eco-" perspective as an orientation that people take when they—like Rickey, Robinson, and Reese—try to move themselves and others from an entrenched way of seeing to the embrace and enactment of the emerging future.

According to Scharmer and Kaufer, "This inner shift, from fighting the old to sensing and presencing an emerging future possibility, is at the core of all deep leadership work today. It's a shift that requires us to expand our thinking from the head to the heart. It is a shift from an *ego*-system awareness that cares about the well-being of oneself to an *eco*-system awareness that cares about the well-being of all, including oneself. . . . When operating with eco-system awareness, we are driven by the concerns and intentions of our emerging or *essential* self—that is, by a concern that is informed by the well-being of the whole."

The authors go on to propose that responding to the emerging future requires an internal shift. Judgments must be suspended and attention refocused. One must let go of the past and embrace the future that is trying to emerge through us. This is what they mean by "presencing" the future. We must become a present manifestation of the future that is trying to unfold. They argue that this is, perhaps, the most important of all leadership capacities.

As we shift from the ego-perspective to the eco-perspective, we become "driven by the concerns and intentions of our emerging or *essential* self—that is, by a concern that is informed by the well-being of the whole."

When we orient to the whole and pursue the best emerging future, we are embracing the highest good and the collective good. As Thoreau suggests, when we make such a choice, a split occurs within us and a better self emerges. It is a self of greater purpose, integrity, empathy, and learning. It is our truest self.

Reese has to make a courageous choice. It is then that he says, "I want these people to see who I really am."

As Reese courageously stands with his arm around Robinson, he is no longer driven by conventional fears. He is acting with purpose and integrity. He is oriented to a higher, collective good. His behavior is a "break from the past." The crowd responds by growing silent. They must make sense of the variation they are beholding. A division occurs in that a few begin to clap. The small boy watches. Cultural change is now spreading beyond the Dodgers to the subset of fans who are inspired by the moral power they behold. It is a meaningful point in the transformation of the United States and the world.

42 is about baseball, and it has grand social implications. The temptation is to label it irrelevant to everyday business. Yet, its implications are for all organizations.

Cultural change occurs when people transcend their fears of conventional pressures and orient to a higher good. Branch Rickey made the courageous choice to live his values and bring forth a future that wanted to emerge through him. He then searched for a Jackie Robinson, a person with the courage to join him in leading social change. As the two moved forward their revolutionary behavior invited others to join, first within the Dodger organization and then outside the Dodger organization.

Please reconsider Thoreau's words from *Civil Disobedience*: "Action from principle, the perception and the performance of right, changes things and relations; it is essentially revolutionary, and does not consist wholly with anything that was. It not only divides states and churches, it divides families; aye, it divides the individual, separating the diabolical in him from the divine."

Success Myths

The shift from the ego-perspective to the eco-perspective can also be seen in some research we conducted on how people define success.[6] We asked people working in professional organizations to produce three stories of times that they were at their best. We then had them analyze what was common across their three stories. We took their data, did some complex analyses, and learned that professional people carry success myths. By myths, we do not mean false beliefs; rather, we mean stories, scripts, narratives, or recipes they are trying to follow. Their myths reflect the orientation they take to the world and to themselves. We found two myths that are especially relevant to the notion of leadership:

MYTH OF INTENSE ACHIEVEMENT

I am at my best when I can create a situation in which I am challenged to demonstrate my ability and obtain appropriate rewards. I take charge of a collective and provide vision and direction. I take an intense action focus, overcoming barriers and emphasizing goal achievement. I am fulfilled when the goal is achieved and the accomplishment recognized. I then turn things over to another.

MYTH OF COLLECTIVE FULFILLMENT

I am at my best when I can do something that fits my values. I am not reward driven, but purpose driven. I serve others. I bring together a collective and help them to develop and embrace a unique vision. I nurture commitment and cohesion through participation and trust building. I stay open to feedback and new alternatives. I feel fulfilled when the group begins to mature. I value the relationships in and the products of the community and stay connected to them.

The majority of the people equate success with the Journey of Intense Achievement. These people want to take charge, provide direction, overcome barriers, and achieve goals. They feel fulfilled when they have accomplished their goals and have received recognition. It would be fair to describe these people as good leaders. They are able to "drive" change, and this is what we tend to look for in leaders—the ability to "get things done."

A smaller percentage of the people are trying to enact the Journey of Collective Fulfillment. These people are driven by a purpose that fits their values. They seek to serve others, to help others find their own vision, and to facilitate participation and trust. They are other-focused team builders. As the collective process unfolds, they stay open to feedback and new alternatives. They are externally open, always learning with others who are learning.

Bilingual

And so there appears to be a differentiation between task and person. The first myth emphasizes goal achievement. The second is more people oriented. It is not unusual for us to ask something like this: "Is your boss a task person or a people person?" This common question assumes two mutually exclusive categories. Research suggests another reality.[7] Transformational leaders (leaders with the ability to effectively change culture) integrate this assumed difference. As suggested in Table 2.2, people with the positive mental map can be both high on task and high on people.

Note that the myth of intense achievement is task driven, but the myth of collective fulfillment is also task focused. The second myth is oriented to achievement, but with less ego. It is an eco-perspective in which people are positively organized.

In this book, we have read of people like Alberto and Gerry, learning to shift from the first to the second orientation. In doing so, they do not lose what they had; instead, they become bilingual. Recall the simple illustration in which Gerry explains the change he made, "Now I spend my time making sure that none of my people act like that. I teach them to listen. They may still have to decide, but first they listen."

As people like Alberto and Gerry evolve, their thinking becomes more complex and more dynamic. They tend to see the organization as a whole, as an evolving system inside a larger evolving context. They become more eco-oriented and strive to establish shared values, while they stimulate the collective pursuit of the common good. By doing these things, they invite the emergence of a more positive organization.

Pursuing the Common Good

I know a consultant from Asia who works with senior business leaders. In his national culture, there is an extreme emphasis on hierarchy and seniority. People in his country are careful to defer to people of higher status.

He told me the story of a large company that was struggling. One reason for the struggle was that the CEO tended to receive little honest feedback from his direct reports. The CEO was operating with many blind spots, and the corporate difficulties were growing in magnitude. The company was moving toward a slow death.

The pain grew so intense that the senior team invited the consultant to work with them. He spent much time with the direct reports. He worked hard to get them to embrace the common good and to take the risk to give the CEO more honest feedback. He trained them on how to be simultaneously respectful and honest.

A two-and-a-half-hour meeting was scheduled. For the first hour and a half, the CEO was uncomfortable. He communicated his discomfort, and his many implicit messages were clearly interpreted by the direct reports. The meeting was teetering on the brink of disaster.

The consultant described his own anxiety. In his country, a man as powerful as the CEO could easily destroy the consultant's career. Performing this sort of intervention was a great risk.

Fortunately, in the last half hour of the meeting, there was a change. The CEO began to see the value in what was taking place, and he opened up. Authentic communication began to flow both ways. People were amazed with the change. The meeting became a positive intervention that led to a lasting shift in the communication patterns of the top management team. The people were becoming more focused on the common good, and the culture was turning more positive.

Surprising Implications

The problem facing this organization is common. Armies of professionals live in fear of speaking truth to power. Unfortunately the pattern is hard to change, because it is driven by self preservation.

In this example, the CEO and his direct reports were unable to do what was required to open the channels of communication because they were ego-driven. They held the conventional mental map, and they feared the risk they perceived to be associated with honest communication. So, despite their positions of authority, no one was able to lead the change process.

This means, that for a period of time, the external consultant actually became the leader of the company. In taking the role, he could not be a conventional consultant. A conventional consultant may have behaved just like the direct reports and the CEO. This consultant had to operate from the positive mental map. He had to have the capacity or the ability to alter the conventional culture by:

- understanding and pursuing his own sense of purpose;
- modeling authenticity and attracting others to authenticity;
- creating belief in the reality of another possibility;
- transcending ego and staying on the journey of collective fulfillment;
- trusting that a more positive culture could emerge; and
- believing that a more positive culture would emerge.

Caring for the Whole

There was considerable risk involved in the case at hand. If the meeting had not turned around in the final half hour, it is a certainty that the consultant would have become the corporate scapegoat. In the days that followed, everything he did would have been redefined as a negative or incompetent influence and numerous stories would be told illustrating his flaws. His career could have been damaged, if not destroyed.

Many people have difficulty with this notion of commitment to the collective purpose. Operating from the self-interested assumptions of the conventional map, one survives by competing for limited resources. Life is a game, and you win by being clever, not by embracing a higher purpose, living with integrity, serving the common good, and cocreating the emerging future.

By operating from an eco-perspective, the consultant was modeling moral power. He was inviting the CEO and the executives into a repaired moral system. As they chose to change, they also moved from the ego-perspective to the eco-perspective. Because they did, they could turn their organization more positive.

Conclusion

In this chapter, we discover some elusive lessons about turning organizations positive. This content is often difficult for people to embrace and accept because it requires the motivation and courage to make self-change, to grow, and to learn. While we fear this process ourselves, we rarely hesitate to ask it of the people who work for us.

From the story of Branch Rickey and Jackie Robinson, we get a fuller understanding of the dynamics of moral power and cultural change. Positive change is not a top-down process. As we pursue the common good, we show people positive deviation. They have to pay attention. As they make choices, they either move toward or away from the highest good.

Research shows that prosocial motivation helps people acquire a more collective and dynamic perspective that is at the heart of the positive mental map. With the more positive perspective, they are better able to pursue the well-being of all, and all includes the self.

The consultant to the top management team was able to initiate a transformation because he had embraced the positive mental map and was aware of his interdependence as part of a larger, dynamic system. He knew that if he had the common good as his highest desire, he was more likely to attract the self-interested executives to a new set of behaviors. He succeeded in his risky endeavor.

The least understood strategy of change is change based on moral power. This potent form of influence becomes available to us as we increase our own commitment to the common good and thus radiate an invitation for others to do likewise.

TOOLS

Quick Assessment: Common Good

Leaders are pursuing their own self-interests.	1 2 3 4 5 6 7 8 9 10	Leaders are pursuing the common good.
We focus on our own personal needs.	1 2 3 4 5 6 7 8 9 10	We focus on winning for the organization.
We are operating in silos.	1 2 3 4 5 6 7 8 9 10	We are all sacrificing for the shared vision.
There is no desire to do a good job.	1 2 3 4 5 6 7 8 9 10	The desire to do a good job is widespread.
Negative peer pressure holds us back.	1 2 3 4 5 6 7 8 9 10	Positive peer pressure moves us forward.

▶ Action Box: Repairing the Moral System

Have your people fill out the Quick Assessment on common good. Collect, and share the results but do not discuss them.

Have your people read this chapter and focus particularly on the case of the consultant who helped turn the senior management team positive. Ask them to answer the following questions.

- What is the common good? (Review the quick assessment.) Give an example.
- What does it mean for an organization to have a moral system? Identify examples.
- The consultant worked with a CEO who did not allow truth to speak to power. Think of an experience that illustrates this same problem? What was the outcome?
- The consultant became the leader of the company. What does this mean? Why was it necessary?
- The consultant had to model moral power and believe that a new culture would unfold in real time. Think of a personal experience that illustrates this principle.
- What is action from principle? Why is it hard? Why is it necessary?

Lead a discussion of these questions. At the end, have everyone write a paragraph that explains how a leader can increase in moral power. Have each person share. Then integrate the insights and outline a strategy for pursuing the common good and elevating the moral health of your organization. Describe how the culture could be different in terms of moral power.

► **Reader Insights**

At the end of this book, you will have the opportunity to fill out the Positive Organization Generator. The first step will be to assess your unit. The second will be to create a vision for your unit. The third will be to find levers or strategies that allow your newly created vision to become a reality. You will find it helpful if you already have some ideas. Please reflect on this chapter and then answer the following two questions.

What new characteristics would I like my unit to have a year from now?

What new ideas do I have for creating a more positive organization?

7 ▲ TRUSTING THE EMERGENT PROCESS

In the first chapter we read about a hospital with a conventional culture. I mentioned that within that hospital there were many people trying to make improvements. The Chair of Surgery was one of the people who wanted a more positive culture.

Working with leaders of the department, we designed a change program, and then I taught the first day of the educational effort. The entire program went well, so the second year they decided to take more surgeons through the process. I was again invited to lead the first day.

In the introduction, the chair of surgery did something that impressed me deeply. He began by reviewing what had happened the previous year. He shared a number of qualitative incidents that were attributable to the program. Then, he listed a number of impressive innovations and positive practices that were direct outcomes of the program. Because the participants had actually seen and benefited from these outcomes, the efficacy of the program was clear.

The chairperson then put up his final slide. It showed an infection. He reminded the surgeons of something they all understood. An infection is a complex system that adapts and grows. It develops as a result of dynamic interactions within the system and without.

He noted that on the first day of the previous year, no one could have imagined the innovations and practices that were now realities. He indicated that those outcomes, like the infection, were emergent: they derived from a change in the connections and conversations that took place in the classroom and, later, in the hospital's offices and hallways. The chairperson did not design them. Much like an infection, the positive culture had emerged as a result of altered interactions, and it would continue to expand as the surgeons continued to internalize the desire for a positive culture and learned to relate in more positive ways.

Everyone in the room grasped the idea of a positive infection. The department was acquiring new capacities, not because of directions from the top, but because people were embracing a higher collective purpose. As they pursued that purpose, they were thinking and interacting in new and authentic ways. The higher quality interactions were giving rise to learning, innovation, and impact.

I was impressed by the simple image that was used to describe the change. The chairperson was accomplishing something that seldom is accomplished. He was helping his people understand self-organization.

Self-Organization

Near the end of the 1982 film *Gandhi*, there is a scene that captures the emergent process. Gandhi announces that he will march 200 miles to the sea. There, in violation of British law, he will make salt. He sees salt as an important symbol. The sea belongs to India and yet Indians are not allowed to make salt. They must buy it from the British. During the march, he calls on all Indians to raise the flag of free India. The British decide to ignore the entire process.[1]

Gandhi begins the march and a foreign correspondent named Vince Walker accompanies him. Walker writes for the *New York Times*. There are some British officers standing nearby. Walker asks if an arrest will end the process.

"Not if they arrest me and a thousand others. It is not only generals who can plan campaigns," Gandhi replies.

Walker then asks, "What if they do not respond?"

Gandhi replies, "It is the function of a civil resistor to provoke and we will continue to provoke until they respond or change the law. They are not in control. We are."

Here we might stop for a moment and think about this exchange. Is Gandhi correct? Is it possible for one man to be in control of the British Empire?

Gandhi is in control. The British are trapped in the assumptions of the conventional mental map, but Gandhi is bilingual. He can see things they cannot see. The blindness of the British is revealed in the next scene.

The march to the sea is successful. World reaction embarrasses the British, and the viceroy meets with his generals. The generals report that salt is being made everywhere. The leaders of congress are selling salt on the streets.

The viceroy orders the process stopped. He wants everyone but Gandhi arrested. The theory is to first cut Gandhi's support out from under him and then deal with him later. In the scene that follows, a general reports that they have arrested nearly 100,000 people. All the leaders and all their families are in jail, and yet the process goes on. The enraged viceroy asks, "Who is leading them?"

The baffled general answers that he does not know.

Here we see the blindness of the British. It is a blindness shared by most of humankind. Living from the conventional mental map, the viceroy and generals assume a hierarchy exists. Their strategy is to remove the leaders from the top of the hierarchy so the organization will crumble. But, when they remove the leaders, something incomprehensible occurs. The movement grows and flourishes.

At this point in the story, Gandhi announces that the next day he will lead a march on the Dharasana Salt Works with the expressed purpose of closing it down. The viceroy, still operating from the conventional mental map, orders Gandhi's arrest and demands that the salt works be kept open at all costs. In the next remarkable scene, hundreds of people line up outside the salt works. A man gives a simple speech. "They expect us to lose heart or to fight back; we will do neither." Then, the first row of men walks slowly into the British lines, where they are clubbed and beaten. The women drag them away and apply first aid. The next row of men walks slowly into the clubs. The brutal process continues.

Through it all, Walker is recording the event. He eventually goes to a phone and dictates the story to the *New York Times*. "Without any hope of escape from injury or death, it went on and on and into the night. Women carried the wounded and broken bodies from the road until they dropped from exhaustion. But still it went on and on. Whatever moral ascendancy the West held was lost here today. India is free. She has taken all that steel and cruelty can give and she has neither cringed nor retreated."

In fact, it would take several more years before the British formally withdrew from India. But this amazing event was the tipping point; it mattered as much as Walker suggests. It took place with Gandhi and all of India's formal leaders in jail. The system of change was emergent and self-organizing. Gandhi understood something the viceroy and the generals could not understand. He knew how to initiate and trust the emergent process.

The Emergent Process

There was a CEO of a large corporation—I will call him Dan—who was a brilliant man with a thirst for action and achievement. During his first five years as CEO, he not only globalized the company but also drove it to impressive levels of profit. Wall Street was delighted. As he entered his sixth year, things grew more difficult. He had stretched the system as far as it would go. As he wrestled with his challenges, he began to talk about the need for values and the commitment to values. He wanted to develop a high-performance culture.[2]

Some people saw this turn as hypocrisy. How could such a hard-nosed and task-focused person talk about values and culture? When I asked Dan about the shift, he told me he continued to be interested in having a high-performance company, but like Alberto and Gerry, Dan made a discovery:

> Sooner or later, every leader comes to understand how little power he or she really has. I will take you back to when this was just a North American business. A person could get things done continuously, consistently. As we became more complex and the environment more intense, it became impossible to get things done through the force of leadership. Everything in my mind has always been so clear and logical. I felt, if we just do what we know how to do every day, this thing will work. I had this grand scheme and grand design and grand vision, and I thought I could articulate it and get people lined up. It did not happen. It absolutely did not happen. I think that I had to come to grips with the fact that it is not enough for me to be committed, to have a plan and understand where we are going. I realized I had to get everyone engaged and committed.

There is an important lesson here. Dan was so brilliant and forceful that, for five years, he was able to "will" his company to success. He then discovered the limitations of power. The conventional mental map suggests that a CEO is a king with unlimited power. Yet, like Alberto and Gerry, Dan discovered that force of leadership and brilliant expertise is not enough. To move to a higher level of corporate performance, Dan had to have a company of "engaged and committed" people. Dan was becoming bilingual. He had just discovered the positive mental map, which added complexity to his current mental map. The complexity allowed him to add new positive characteristics from Figure 1.1— characteristics that were opposing his current value set. Opening himself to these opposing, positive values started a new vision of how he could create a more positive organization. This meant that he was ready to learn about the emergent process.

Shortly after making that statement, there was a meeting of the company's top 100 leaders. The objective was to deal with some difficult issues around collaboration and compensation. A gifted HR leader designed the meeting. He recognized the difference between a technical problem that is solved through the application of existing knowledge and an adaptive problem that is solved through collective learning.[3] He indicated that the real issues would be put on the table, and an authentic conversation would occur.

Dan was conceptually committed to the process. We all knew, though, that when the inevitable conflict began to surface, he would have a strong temptation to take control. The HR leader explained that Dan needed to stop himself from taking control. Several people would be working as facilitators and would help the participants own their conflict and keep moving. He told Dan to "trust the process."

The HR leader then went out and had a coin made. The coin said, "Trust the process." He told Dan he needed to put it in his pocket, and, whenever he wanted to take control, he needed to squeeze the coin and hold back.

The issue of collaboration and compensation was introduced at the meeting of the top 100 leaders. The major issue was that people were compensated according to the continent on which they worked, and it was causing silo behavior. The company was not functioning as a whole. As the issue was addressed, the predicted conflict emerged. During one break, a very concerned participant told me he had never seen the company so divided; he was fearful of what might happen next. Teams continued to meet and discuss the issue. In the afternoon, we assembled as a large group. One team articulated what kind of collaboration was necessary and proposed a radical shift in the compensation system. Another team made a similar proposal. In a short time, there was a consensus. The people had embraced a shift that was far beyond what Dan would have dared to propose.

Later, the HR leader asked Dan what he was feeling when the conflict was high. Dan said, "I was squeezing that coin so hard, I think I bent it."

Trusting the Process

What Gandhi understood deeply, Dan was learning. To embrace the positive mental map is to see the organization not only as a stable hierarchy but also as a constantly changing social network in which everyone has information and influence. The people in the network have the potential to embrace the common good, make spontaneous contributions, feel confident, seek growth, overcome constraints, expand their roles, express their authentic voice, see and seize new opportunities, build social networks, nurture high-quality connections, embrace feedback, and exceed expectations.

At the heart of the *conventional* mental map is the assumption of knowing. An expert solves a technical problem by applying knowledge. At the heart of the *positive* mental map is the assumption of collective learning. People pursue a purpose they do not yet know how to accomplish. As they move forward, they learn and adapt, eventually producing a new level of understanding and order. For someone living from the conventional mental map, emergence is difficult to comprehend, and trusting the process is nearly impossible. Consider an illustration from the book *Life at the Edge of Chaos: Creating the Quantum Organization*.[4]

In the book, author Mark Youngblood tells the story of a warehouse in Dallas that was being inventoried for the first time. Youngblood was a consultant leading the initiative. Sally was the manager representing the client organization. Youngblood knew that the process of counting and reconciliation would border on chaos. He expected the individual team members to think for themselves. He expected the team to move forward—improvising and learning constantly.

The process started well, but then a very uncomfortable Sally stepped in and took control. She became the centralizing mechanism demanding that each person report to her and follow her direction. At first this caused things to go smoother. But then, the number of problems began to expand. Each one was unique and took considerable time to resolve. People began waiting around while Sally solved their problems. Soon she was overwhelmed and then she collapsed in exhaustion.

When she was no longer in control, team members returned to the original approach. Empowered actors combined in the process of collective learning. By morning, the project was complete.

In the story, Sally comes off as a kind of villain. Uncomfortable with what she perceives as chaos, she seizes control. In fact, what she did is what the viceroy would have done, it is what Dan would have done, and it is what almost all of us would have done. Her behavior is a reflection of the conventional mental map. She could not conceive or trust the process of self-organization.

Recognizing Emergence

Learning to understand and trust the emergent process is not easy. Consider an educational exercise that I run with some regularity: You are among 40 other people who have come to a seminar at the University of Michigan's Ross School of Business. Everyone there is a stranger to everyone else. I put you in four small groups. I pass out blindfolds and you put one on.[5]

I tell you that in a few minutes I am going to send you to a destination point somewhere else in the building. Your job is to find your way there as a team—but with your blindfolds in place at all times. Once you get to your assigned space, there will be a set of materials on the floor. As a team, you must find all the materials and assemble them into a single object. With blindfolds in place, you must figure out what that object is and build it with quality. When you are done, you will return to the room where we are now meeting. When everyone on your team is sitting in the correct chair, you may then take off your blindfold. You have three minutes to plan your strategy.

When the three minutes are up, each team is assigned its destination point and is told to begin. Like the blind leading the blind, you and your team members join hands and begin groping your way toward the assigned destination. Uncertainty is rampant, and progress is slow and messy, but eventually, and after some mistakes, you do arrive at your destination. Your team now confronts a number of complex problems:

- How do you find the materials?
- How do you figure out what the object is?
- How do you assemble a complex object you cannot see?

For a while, you engage in the chaotic assembly process. At last, your team concludes the task. You join hands and grope your way back to your starting point. With everyone back in the right chair, you remove your blindfolds. You and everyone else on your team stand up and begin slapping high fives. I tell your group to go back to the room where you previously met and see your product for the first time. As a group, you head over to the place where you built the object. There, your team circles the object. There are more high fives and excited talk about what has occurred. Each of the other teams has the same experience.

I next ask the groups to reconstruct the history of their team and list what they believe were the keys to their success. Your group reports the following: "We talked about our assignment and then developed a plan. We appointed a leader. We executed our plan and then returned successfully. We had a common goal; luckily, we had a person with some expertise on building such objects; we had a good plan and an effective leader; we stayed within our plan; we had a sense of urgency; we had communication, trust, and teamwork; we listened well; we were persistent."

Most people going through this process will interpret the experience as being a really good team-building session. They don't fully appreciate what actually happened. In the debriefing, I typically make the following three points:

1. The claim about expertise is wrong. There are groups that end up with no object expert; yet, they also complete the task. Expertise is helpful, but it is not a prerequisite because human groups know how to learn.

2. The claim about appointing a leader is accurate but misleading. Even though some groups appointed a leader and the leader provided some direction, the leadership was not centralized. It moved constantly from person to person as was appropriate; no one controlled the shifting process.
3. The claim that you all had a plan and then went out and executed it is a distortion. The process was very messy and you made endless mistakes. All you had was a directive, a set of strangers in a new relationship, and a set of feedback loops that emerged once you started to move. Through trial and error, you learned and you created the future that is now part of your past.

At first, these observations seem confusing but then they start to make sense. There was a very messy process that went unreported, a process that counterbalanced planning, control, and execution. In reflecting on the process, however, the group tended to underreport the messy learning process.

This is important because in life we do experience the emergent process. A need emerges, it becomes a purpose, we join with others in learning by trial and error, we authentically communicate what we are learning, and the group evolves until it fails or acquires the capacity to succeed. Then, operating from the conventional mental map, we give a linear and hierarchical account of what took place. The conventional mental map is so strong that, even when we experience the emergent process, we have difficulty seeing it. This makes it difficult to learn how to nurture and trust the process.

Nurturing and Trusting Emergence

My son Ryan is a management professor at the University of Louisville. Ryan and I worked together on cultural change for a large group of organizational development practitioners. Our objective was to help them understand the elusive concepts of collective intelligence and the emergence of new capacities. Ryan put up a slide that presented a mini case study:

Kurt Wright was a consultant for a company working on a $100 million, 60-month software development project for the government. There were 400 engineers working on the project. Thirty-eight months had already passed, and the project was 18 months behind schedule. A clause in the contract stated that if the project were 18 months behind at the 48-month milestone, the company would suffer a $30 million penalty. Managers and employees were frightened about losing $30 million because of the impact it would have on their company, their unit, and their jobs. Stress was beginning to escalate.[6]

Ryan asked the group to suggest strategies on how to change this situation. The participants made many suggestions. Most had to do with analysis and problem solving. Ryan listened and then shared what Wright actually did:

Wright began asking people in the hallways and in meetings, 'What will it take to finish this project a week early?' Early on, this question angered many people. He was summoned into managers' offices and told that he was losing his credibility and would get himself in trouble if he did not stop. He listened politely, went back into the halls, and kept asking the same question. Wright finished his work in six weeks, using only $90,000 of his $150,000 budget. The project was completed on time (in 60 months), $15 million under budget. If you include the $30 million that the company did not lose at the 48-month mark, Wright's simple question was worth $45,060,000.

Ryan remarked that this story seemed like a fantasy. Many skeptical heads were nodding. Ryan then suggested that the members of the audience work a little harder, dig a little deeper. He wanted them to challenge their conventional assumptions.

At this point, Ryan changed the direction of the meeting. He focused on the anger that had grown among the people in the case study over Wright's question. After a pause, insightful answers began to flow. Here are the things the participants said. As you read the list, try to imagine the underlying dynamics that were starting to occur in the audience that was giving these answers.

- They were busy and feeling stressed. Wright's question was a disruption to their narrow, problem-solving focus. It was a source of more stress.

- They felt helpless. They did not know the answer. If they had known it, they would already be pursuing it. Wrights question was exposing their ignorance and inability. It was embarrassing.
- Engineers are already behind schedule. This negative organizational state was probably within their comfort zone. The question was threatening because it invited them to step outside it. They would rather live in the stress of a failing organization because it was something they were used to. They did not want to learn and change.
- The participants live in a technical world. They believed they were paying Wright to provide technical answers to their problems. Instead, he was wasting their time with an abstract question. They were too busy to waste time like that.
- They were all sensing failure and were pursuing their self-interests. They were forming silos and tacitly preparing self-protective arguments to shift blame. By posing the question, Wright was asking them to contemplate the collective good. But no one was oriented toward the collective good. They were all governed by their own self-interest.
- Wright was a consultant. Having a consultant was a sign that the company's leaders did not know how to lead change in their own organization. Wright was thus an implicit symbol of their shame and hopelessness. Because of such assumptions, people love to hate consultants, and if a consultant does something out of the ordinary, they will informally self-organize to "kill" the consultant. Their anger was the start of the assassination process.
- The question posed accountability. It suggested they were responsible. When disempowered people face accountability, they get angry. Most people are disempowered. They live in a reactive state.

As the audience provided these insightful answers, something subtle began to happen. They were changing from an audience to a group. First, they were productively pursuing the discussion of a topic they found interesting. Everyone was respectfully listening, and the answers were increasingly thoughtful. In interacting, they were collectively creating new knowledge.

By engaging in this discussion, the audience of strangers was becoming a more productive, authentic, empathetic, and adaptive group. They were operating with increased capacity and were in the process of creating a positive culture of their own. There were more positive emotions in the room, and positive emotions give rise to positive thoughts and behaviors. Each person was part of a highly functioning, emergent whole. Together, they were having experiences they could not have had individually. In this condition of increased positivity, they were more open and ready to explore why Wright's strategy worked.

When Ryan then asked about Wright's strategy, they began to share more insights:

- If Wright had told them what to do, they would have resisted. In asking a question, Wright was moving them from knowing to inquiry. He was also disturbing their comfort zone, inviting them outside their current assumptions. It made them uneasy. They wanted him to stop.
- In asking the question, Wright was not acting like a manager of engineers. He was acting like a leader of people. His question was a question of higher purpose. The question suggested a better collective future. To ask people to imagine such a future is to suggest an image worthy of sacrifice. He was inviting them into the sacred space where new things can happen.
- By proceeding in the face of their anger, Wright was showing a level of commitment they did not expect. By modeling vision and courage, he was demonstrating a belief in their potential. Such virtuous effort can become a magnet that draws out people's latent virtue. Wright was embodying the collective good, and it was an invitation to collective commitment.
- In posing a question rather than a solution, he was avoiding the hierarchical, expert role. He was inviting them into a social relationship in which he would be their equal in learning their way into the future. Here again, he was honoring their agency, and he was allowing them the private space to think for themselves.

- His question demonstrated a belief in the process of self-organization and cocreation. He did not have to design and control the
creation of a new organization. It would emerge spontaneously
as each actor pursued the group's shared purpose. In pursuing the
common good, they would, without hierarchical direction,
cocreate a new and better system.

I found these responses inspiring. Few people understand the emergent
process. This group was collectively articulating it. Something else was
also happening.

Ryan was stimulating emergence. He was facilitating a change in the
state of the group. By moving the group into the process of cocreation,
the people were better able to make sense of the positive organizing process that the Wright case illustrates. In doing this kind of work, Ryan
was attempting to bring about the actualization of the elusive concept
we were trying to teach, the emergence of collective intelligence. How
did it happen?

In asking his question, Wright was using inquiry to provoke the system. The provoked agents began to act in new ways. As the process continued new collective patterns emerged. A systemic solution evolved from
the bottom up.

As Ryan shared the case and facilitated the discussion, he also provoked individual thinking and sharing. As commitment, authenticity,
trust, and sharing took place, the audience became a learning organization with increased collective intelligence. They were creating a positive
organization.

Conclusion

Emergence and self-organization are hard to understand.[7] Facilitating
emergence is even harder to do. It requires that we let go of our expert
role and trust the people who are working on the issue. It can feel chaotic in the beginning, so it requires patience and great confidence.

The illustrations in this chapter show us that positive patterns can
emerge and spread through an organization in an organic way. While
many leaders struggle to learn how to facilitate the emergent process,
others become adept at positive provocation and facilitation. The challenge of this chapter is to be sensitive to emergence. We need to recognize

it, understand it, provoke it, and then trust the process. This may be the hardest of all the concepts in this book but it opens the door to more effectively leading change.

As we have seen throughout this text, the movement from the conventional to positive mental map requires transformative or deep learning, a change in basic assumptions. This process is not easy. It requires experiential learning. One purpose of this book is to entice you into and coach you through such learning. With that purpose in mind, we now turn to the Positive Organization Generator.

TOOLS

Quick Assessment: Emergence

We are fearful of trying new things.	1 2 3 4 5 6 7 8 9 10	We are empowered to try new things.
We infect each other with cynicism.	1 2 3 4 5 6 7 8 9 10	We infect each other with enthusiasm.
Leadership is in one person.	1 2 3 4 5 6 7 8 9 10	Leadership moves from person to person.
We are micro-managed.	1 2 3 4 5 6 7 8 9 10	We initiate without management direction.
We fail to meet our own expectations.	1 2 3 4 5 6 7 8 9 10	We exceed our own expectations.

► *Action Box: The Emergent Process*[8]

This exercise is designed to help your people learn to lead a meeting where emergence might occur. Have your people fill out the Quick Assessment. Share the results, but do not discuss them at this time.

Have participants review the list under Step 1: Preparation. As they do, they should record their impressions or ideas.

When they are done reading and recording, hold a discussion. Have people share their impressions about each principle. Record the shared impressions. Then collectively create a realistic template for how to provoke and trust the emergent process in a meeting.

Step 1: Preparation
- Identify a challenge your unit is currently facing and think deeply about it. Reflect on "all" the people involved and remind yourself of "all" values, beliefs, assumptions, roles, relationships, and structures that may have to change. Recognize that people will naturally want to "deny" the need for change.
- Turn the problem statement into a purpose statement—a positive outcome to achieve. Remember the Kurt Wright example: "What will it take to finish this project a week early?" He shifted his people from problem solving to the pursuit of purpose. How can you do the same?

Step 2: Team Meeting
- Start by focusing the people on the positive. Ask the people what they most love about the organization, and then list their answers. Building the list will change the emotional climate in the room.
- In terms of the pressing problem, ask them what result they want to create and help them come to a potent statement of purpose. Do not proceed until everyone feels the purpose statement is authentic.
- Be high on task and high on support. Keep inviting the people to move forward. Help them to keep surfacing the most difficult issues. (Surfacing conflict is necessary, only then can it be transformed.)
- Constantly revisit and clarify the purpose that makes the process worthwhile. But do not take ownership or apply your expertise. Continually empower the people and let them own the process.

- Be strongly authentic. Reveal your vulnerability. Build trust and authenticity. Evaluate for authenticity, and invite the group to return to authenticity. In the darkest moments, trust the process.
- If these steps seem too unnatural, bring in an experienced "process" consultant to execute the above. Pay attention and learn from the consultant's example. Everyone in your unit needs to learn to facilitate the emergent process. Fleeing from the work of facilitation is a leadership failure.

► *Reader Insights*

At the end of this book, you will have the opportunity to fill out the Positive Organization Generator. The first step will be to assess your unit. The second will be to create a vision for your unit. The third will be to find levers or strategies that allow your newly created vision to become a reality. You will find it helpful if you already have some ideas. Please reflect on this chapter and then answer the following two questions.

What new characteristics would I like my unit to have a year from now?

What new ideas do I have for creating a more positive organization?

8 ▲ USING THE POSITIVE ORGANIZATION GENERATOR

I met with the top 200 people of a large corporation. Their industry was turning upside down, and they were facing a rapidly evolving external world. They had spent the previous day conceptualizing their strategic future, and now they wanted me to help them think about their culture and how to insure the implementation of their new strategy.

I opened by telling them I believed that, within two hours, we could actually initiate culture change in their company. I said this with complete confidence; they, of course, "knew" that it was impossible. An outsider cannot initiate culture change—especially not in two hours.

In the first hour, we had an unusually honest discussion about leadership and the nature of organizational change. We explored the fact that instead of moving toward an ever more positive culture where people sacrifice for the common good, most organizations maintain conventional cultures full of self-interested people. The people continually splinter, and the organization moves toward a slow death.

I asked the participants to reflect on the strategy work they did the day before, take everything they heard in the discussion of their future, and reduce it to three to five bullet points specifying what was going to be demanded of their particular unit. This took two minutes.

Next, we looked at the Positive Organization Generator, the tool you will find in the appendix. Using the first part of the tool, the participants had some time to diagnose the current culture of their unit and to specify what their desired culture looks like.

Finally, we looked at a list of 100 positive practices from other companies. I explained the following:

- This is a list of 100 practices. The organizations claim that these positive practices changed their culture for the better. We do not know if the claims are true, but it does not matter. Our objective is not to adopt or imitate the practices. Instead, you will use the practices as inspiration for the creation of your own, new practices.
- The first step is for you to examine the 100 practices and identify the ones that most interest you.
- Now, focusing only on the practices of most interest, ask this crucial question, "How can I *reinvent* this practice?" Reinvent means to recreate, reconceive, redesign, or refashion. *You are not to adopt the practice, you are to reinvent it.*
- In reinventing the most interesting practices, the objective is to create new practices that meet three criteria.
  - First, the practice is reinvented to your unique situation.
  - Second, the reinvention process is real; you feel genuinely excited about the prospect of implementing the practice.
  - Third, it is a practice you can implement without asking permission.

With these instructions, they went to work. When they finished the effort, I asked them to share their new practices with each other. As I walked by one table, one of the participants uttered an interesting statement. He exclaimed:

WE REALLY *CAN* MAKE CHANGE!

As I later debriefed the larger group, I cited that comment and asked if anyone else shared his feeling. Many hands went up. These were the leaders of the company, and yet they were surprised to learn that they could make change. I suggested that in doing the exercise we were moving from assumptions of constraint to assumptions of constraint and possibility.

One man raised his hand. He could hardly contain himself as he described a new way to positively engage both customers and suppliers.

Others wrote down his idea. We followed this with more sharing. When we reflected on what was actually happening in the room, the participants said:

- We are coming up with ideas that will make our individual areas more positive.
- We are creating ideas that we really believe in.
- We are getting ideas from each other.

I asked how many believed they would actually go back to their own units and do something. All the hands went up. I asked them what would happen if each one only implemented half of their ideas. Someone responded, "That is a lot of positive change."

They all believed that an organization is a hierarchy of authority and that change happens from the top down. Yet, I was suggesting that an organization is also a network of relationships and that change can be an emergent process that flows from the bottom up. It can happen without any centralized coordinating mechanism. It can emerge from the enactment of new practices.

> I told them that as each of them implemented their positive practices, the successful practices would have the potential to create a ripple effect. Despite conventional resistance, very few new practices were likely to travel from unit to unit. However, if someone in a key position became a facilitator of assessment and sharing, the practices could spread in larger numbers and with more impact. When the change process is courageously initiated from below and courageously supported from above, learning and development is accelerated.

As I was leaving the meeting, many people wanted to talk. What impressed me the most was how grounded the conversations were. Each person shared specific things they planned to do. As I went out the door, I felt confident that we had initiated the process of elevating the culture. For it to continue, much more would have to be done, but the people were seeing new possibilities and had invented their own practices, and most were eager to go home and implement them. Six months later I was invited back to repeat the process with a large number of people in a different part of the organization.

The Origin of the Tool

The positive organization generator was born out of frustration.

Whenever I would spend a week introducing executives to the concepts in this book, they would tend to show interest and excitement. Yet at the end of a week a strange thing would consistently happen. I would put them in groups and ask them to generate a list of new, positive practices that they could go home and implement. The output would be surprisingly unimpressive. I could not figure out why.

I watched this happen many times. Then one day a simple sentence changed my perspective. I was sharing some material when a participant became unusually excited. Based on an exercise we had just completed, he could see how he could use positive symbols to further his objectives. He excitedly spoke of an upcoming meeting and specified specific things he could do. Suddenly he stopped, his energy level dropped for a moment, and he said softly, "I know it sounds corny but it might work." I glanced around the room, people were looking down.

As I stood there I had an important insight. The practices that emerge from the positive mental map are always foreign to the conventional mental map. People know that the existing organization culture is predisposed to reject and resist movement to the positive. The resistance often occurs in stages, first humor, then rational argument and then moral indignation and rejection. Everyone knows that making real change is dangerous.

In the end, professionals are not much different from high school students. At all levels we live in fear of failure and social rejection. The word "corny" is symbolic of the fear. No one wants to be laughed at, no one wants to fail. Given these feelings, people, even at the highest levels, carry assumptions of constraint. Recall the earlier statement made by the surprised executive who had just completed the positive Organization Generator.

"We really can make change!"

What does this sentence tell us about his assumptions?

People, even in high positions, tend regularly to slip into the conventional mental map. Teaching executives the principles of positive leadership and positive organization is insufficient. I had to do more for the people in my classes. I had to help the executives not only see possibility, I also had to help them believe, create and act. It was shortly after the emergence of this insight that the Positive Organization Generator was created.

The Name of the Tool

The Positive Organization Generator is a tool designed to help people create practices that they believe in and desire to implement within their own zone of control. The name of the tool is important. Many people ask; "Why don't you call it the Positive Practices Generator?"

The answer is that positive cultures emerge from new positive practices. The continuous introduction of new, positive practices is what generates a more positive organization.

The conventional mental map assumes that change derives from a formal plan conceived and implemented in a linear, top-down fashion. Recall Unit 5 of Hospital 2. In a conventional organization with conventional subunits, a very positive unit emerged. Unit 5 was not a product of a plan conceived and implemented from the top and it emerged despite widespread pressures to be conventional. It emerged because a woman conceived of, introduced, and nurtured new practices that were far outside the conventional model and conventional pressures.

The Positive Organization Generator is a tool designed to help you create new practices in your zone of control. Contrary to conventional thinking, the assumption is that no matter what is going on around you, you can still create a positive organization.

The Output

The Positive Organization Generator is designed to help you create a product. The tool has several steps. In those steps you will take an assessment, create a vision, review the practices, and select the practices you like, and then re-invent them and complete an action plan. Here is an example of an output created by a branch manager in a large bank.

MY VISION AND POSITIVE PRACTICE PLAN
An Example

My Vision

(This vision is written from one year in the future. The author writes as if she is looking back and describing something that has already occurred.)

A year ago I decided to emphasize three values: vision and purpose; respect and trust; profit and wealth, and I created a set of new, positive practices. Today I returned to work after being away for a week. I walked in the door and everyone was fully engaged. Even though I was gone for week, they were able to function without me. Because they fully understood our shared purpose, they could make the decisions they needed to make. In the first meeting of the day we examined some data that showed that in the previous quarter, a serious mistake occurred. We surfaced the mistake, analyzed it, and conceptualized how to prevent it in the future. There was no finger pointing. People trusted and respected each other. They were able to stick together even though something went wrong. In the meeting we moved on to review the profit report. As we expected, we had outperformed every other branch in the bank. An assistant branch manager, who used to be a wet blanket, told us several stories about feedback from excited customers and then offered some ideas on how to get better. At the end of the day the phone rang. It was a vice president asking if he could bring a group of new branch managers to observe us for a day. He wanted them to see what is possible. I went out the door with a smile on my face.

MY POSITIVE PRACTICE PLAN

	My Customized Practices	Start Date
1	**Articulation of Purpose:** I am going to interview all my people and ask them what they think the purpose of our branch is. I am also going to interview key people from outside. I will consolidate and share all the insights I gain. Working with the team I am going to develop a purpose statement and make it the center of all we do. I am then going to help each person understand how their role aligns with the purpose. I will also clarify how pursuing our purpose links with profit. Every time a question comes to me, I will ask what our purpose and our desire for profit would suggest. I will expect them to answer.	February
2	**Idea Generation:** We have a defunct idea generation process. It was always about how to save money. I am going to renew it but it will be about how to grow the people and the business. If someone initiates a good idea that person will be on the project team no matter how low their position is.	March
3	**Black holes:** I am going to identify the de-energizers. I will make it clear that there is a technical portion of the job and a human portion and that everybody is expected to be a positive energizer. I will help the black holes change or help them find a new place to work.	April
4	**Leadership Improvement:** Each quarter I will share a leadership challenge. I will distribute the cards from the Positive Leadership game (an exercise she participated in during her week of executive education).[1] I will ask my people to form triads and come up with suggestions. I will record their ideas. The next quarter I will report back on how I implemented their ideas. After several iterations I will invite them to follow my example. I will invite them to model the same vulnerability and engage in the same improvement process with their people.	May

MY POSITIVE PRACTICE PLAN (Continued)

	My Customized Practices	Start Date
5	Profit Month: I will introduce the notion of "Profit Month." I will do the conceptual introduction three months before profit month. The goal of profit month will be to double the best single month we ever had. We will spend three months preparing. Every week each team will submit ideas on how to prepare for and make profit month a success. Each idea will be rated by every other team. We will keep team standings for quality of contribution. At the end the best team with the best contributions will get significant recognition. During profit month the most profitable team will also get significant recognition. There will be, however, an actual financial bonus that will go to everyone in the branch based on the percentage of collective profit improvement by our entire unit. The following month we will do an analysis of what we learned and what we should do differently in the future so as to continually increase profit.	June

This action plan came about as the result of a careful process followed by the branch manager—the same process now captured in the Positive Organization Generator. She reviewed dozens of examples of positive practices, from which she selected five that were meaningful to her. Then she reinvented them to fit her current situation. Here are the five positive practices and the five reinventions:

Positive Practice 1: Creating Purpose and Passion: To unify The VW brand, the CMO learned German, interviewed 100 staff, traveled the globe to discover shared, key points of pride, used wide involvement to create a centralized brand and tied it to the points of pride.

Reinvention 1: Articulation of Purpose: I am going to interview all my people and ask them what they think the purpose of our branch is. I am also going to interview key people from outside. I will consolidate and share all the insights I gain. Working with the team I am going to develop a purpose statement and make it the center of all we do. I am then going to help each person understand how their role aligns with the purpose. I will also clarify how pursuing our purpose links with profit. Every time a question comes to me, I will ask what our purpose and our desire for profit would suggest. I will expect them to answer.

Positive Practice 2: Idea Market: Rite-Solutions puts new product ideas into an internal market place. Each idea begins trading at $10. Each employee has $10,000 of play money to invest. Employees can also sign up to work on a proposed project. If an ideas turns into a real product, play money can be redeemed for cash.

Reinvention 2: Idea Generation: We have a defunct idea generation process. It was always about how to save money. I am going to renew it but it will be about how to grow the people and the business. If someone initiates a good idea that person will be on the project team no matter how low their position is.

Positive Practice 3: Caring for the Whole: Robert W. Baird & Co. has a "no assholes policy." In selection they look for the ability to care. They value doing things the "right way, all the time," and they have extreme on-boarding and mentoring policies designed to socialize people into the highly cohesive culture.

Reinvention 3: Black holes: I am going to identify the de-energizers. I will make it clear that there is a technical portion of the job and a human portion and that everybody is expected to be a positive energizer. I will help the black holes change or help them find a new place to work.

Positive Practice 4: Servant Leadership: People at the Motely Fool refer to the organization as a "low-rarchy." This is a reminder that everyone is a leader and senior people exist to serve the needs of their associates throughout the organization.

Reinvention 4: Leadership Improvement: Each quarter I will share a leadership challenge. I will distribute the cards from The Positive Leadership Game (an exercise she participated in during her week of executive education). I will ask my people to form triads and come up with suggestions. I will record their ideas. The next quarter I will report back on how I implemented their ideas. After several iterations I will invite them to follow my example. I will invite them to model the same vulnerability and engage in the same improvement process with their people.

Positive Practice 5: Profitability Training: Keller Williams Realty has a training program for agents to increase profitability. For seven weeks, there is intense pursuit of leads and of business growth opportunities. There is continuous emphasis on mindset, language, and techniques and big results. Graduates of this program increased their closed transactions by 50 percent and increased their income by 114 percent.

Reinvention 5: Profit Month: I will introduce the notion of "Profit Month." I will do the conceptual introduction three months before profit month. The goal of profit month will be to double the best single month we ever had. We will spend three months preparing. Every week each team will submit ideas on how to prepare for and make profit month a success. Each idea will be rated by every other team. We will keep team standings for quality of contribution. At the end the best team with the best contributions will get significant recognition. During profit month the most profitable team will also get significant recognition. There will be, however, an actual financial bonus that will go to everyone in the branch based on the percentage of collective profit improvement by our entire unit. The following month we will do an analysis of what we learned and what we should do differently in the future so as to continually increase profit.

Excitement

Every plan is unique. Yours should not look like the plan of anyone else. The key here is the reinvention process. You need to create practices you believe in, that you are excited to implement. If you are excited and the practice does not work, you are much more likely to learn and try again. It is through trial and error learning that most change happens. You will not lead real change unless you really care.

Using the Positive Organization Generator

The paper version of the tool follows in the next section. We have also created a free online tool that you can use and share with your teams. It can be found on the Lift Exchange portal at: http://www.LiftExchange .com/Generator. I hope it will prove useful to you as you strive to create a more positive organization.

▲ APPENDIX

The Positive Organization Generator

Note: This instrument is available to you in digital form at the following link: http://LiftExchange.com/Generator

Chapter 8 was about how to use the Positive Organization Generator. If you have not read it, we encourage you to do so.

Step One
Assessment

We introduced you to Figure 1.1 in chapter 1 of this book. This tool can help us think and act in more complex and positive ways. It can help us to recognize where our organization is and where it is that we want it to go. We return to it now with a way to use it to do a rough assessment of your company.

Shade (or circle) the positive and negative characteristics of your organization. This will help you become conscious of present strengths and weaknesses and the tensions between them. The more positives you have marked, the better off you are. As you identify weaknesses in the negative zone, examine the positive opposite and imagine changes that would create a positive tension between these opposing characteristics. You should use the assessment to think about the vision you want to create for your organization in step 2 of this tool.

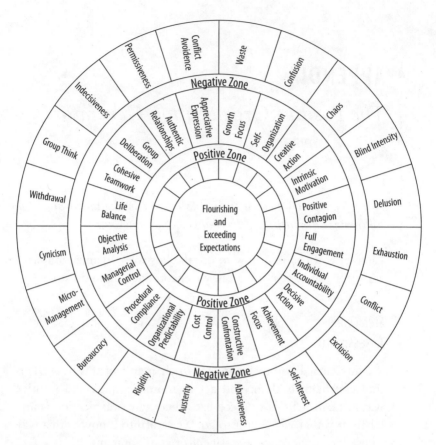

FIGURE 1.1 A Framework of Organizational Tensions

Step Two
Vision Building

Directions: In order to create a more positive organization, think about the following items and then write your vision. Pretend that in one hand you are holding your current organization and in the other you are holding your organization as you would like it to be next year. As you look from the one to the other, you are amazed by the differences you see between them. Your future organization is incredibly positive and has accomplished feats you would never have dreamed possible within the current organization.

What is it about your future organization that is so different? How do people relate to each other? What ways are they flourishing? What is the culture around decisions, risks, and innovations? What leadership styles are being enacted? What is motivating people? What behaviors are rewarded, and how are they rewarded?

1. Review your assessment.
2. Review the vision notes that you wrote at the end of each chapter. Use those insights to consider the vision you want to write for your team.
3. Consider the five levers that were discussed in this book: Creating a Sense of Purpose, Nurturing Authentic Conversations, Seeing Possibility, Embracing the Common Good, and Trusting the Emergent Process. Which of those levers could help your team to be more positive?
4. Write a paragraph describing how you and the people on your team will be behaving if your vision comes to pass. You can review the sample vision in Chapter 8 for help.

My Vision of My Unit

Key Insights from the Assessment and the Chapter Notes:

My Vision:

Step Three
The Positive Organization Generator
Reviewing Positive Practices

Here you will find over 100 unusual, positive practices from real organizations. The practices have been categorized by the five levers in this book. Using your vision as a guide, you can select which of the categories you'd like to review first. Feel free to review only those categories that directly connect to your vision (or to go through all of them). Do not dwell on any items, simply record your first response by writing the number that best reflects your level of interest in the practice in the left-hand column.

CREATING A SENSE OF PURPOSE

Based on the following scale, indicate your interest in each of these practices.

Uninterested 1 2 3 4 5 6 7 8 9 10 Interested

1. _____ Tangible Vision: Microsoft's vision is: "A personal computer in every home running Microsoft software." This simple, concrete, visual statement allows every employee to continually link their work back to a common and understandable aspiration.[1]

2. _____ Looking Ahead: Ford holds a Business Plan Review meeting. The global business environment is monitored at many levels, so everyone is looking ahead at developing trends and has a shared understanding of what might happen, particularly to customers.[2]

3. _____ Higher Purpose: Cascade Engineering has a purpose beyond profit. In one case, they greatly persevered in learning how to turn state and federal aid recipients into employees. This has been recognized by the White House, and the company now reaps unforeseen benefits.[3]

4. _____ Higher Values: Chipotle put a new emphasis on the humane raising of livestock and the employment of organic produce. This has increased revenue for suppliers and satisfaction for health-conscious consumers. Competitive advantage rose, and profits went into double digits.[4]

5. _____ Allowing Project Selection: At Facebook, new employees go through a seven-week boot camp. In the process, they learn of new projects that are about to start, and they are free to choose which one they want to work on. They are placed on the project whether there is room for them or not.[5]

6. _____ Community Service Week: Every year, FedEx employees participate in the FedEx Cares Program. Employees spend a week as volunteers in some form of community development. This increases personal and collective meaning and builds stronger ties to the community.[6]

7. _____ Global Service: IBM hosts a Smarter Cities Challenge program in which the company sends teams of employees around the world to help address community issues. Employees are strongly in favor of the program and often express that it is one of the most rewarding experiences of their career.[7]

8. _____ Shared Purpose: Deloitte has a recognition program centered on the company's mission. When employees are recognized, their accomplishments are linked back to some aspect of the desired collective outcomes. This creates a culture that supports shared purposes.[8]

9. _____ Profit Sharing: Assurance Agency has a profit sharing program based on the achievement of four goals. Two are financial and two are cultural. It is clear to all that both performance and values matter.[9]

10. _____ Selection on Purpose: In searching for employees, The Motley Fool looks for people of purpose, who are willing to learn and are unafraid to fail publicly.[10]

NURTURING AUTHENTIC CONVERSATIONS

Based on the following scale, indicate your interest in each of these practices.

Uninterested 1 2 3 4 5 6 7 8 9 10 Interested

1. _____ Quality Feedback: Ernst & Young did an analysis of their highest performing departments. The commonality was quality feedback. They worked on improving the quality of feedback to all employees, and engagement increased dramatically.[11]

2. _____ Authentic Customer Relations: Kimpton Hotels seeks to create authentic relationships among employees and between employees and guests by encouraging employees to show up and be who they really are. They are trained to celebrate their differences.[12]

3. _____ Open Book Finance: At Zingerman's, employees are trained in open book finance so everyone has the full financial picture and knows how they can best help the company succeed financially.[13]

4. _____ Rumor Game: The Scooter Store plays the "Rumor Game" during company rallies. The CEO asks employees to raise a recently circulating rumor that they would like to know the truth about. He rewards volunteers with gifts.[14]

5. _____ Postmortems: DreamWorks seeks to learn from mistakes, encourages risk-taking, and fosters innovation. The company carries out "postmortems" to learn from the past and prevent the repeat of mistakes. The focus is on improving processes, not people.[15]

6. _____ Learning Versus Blame: In seeking to build a culture of safety, Pacific Gas and Electric turned their focus from placing blame to a positive focus on learning and improvement. Employees began to step forward, sharing and learning from mistakes.[16]

7. _____ Culture Councils: At Quantum Health, councils on the culture are held twice a year. A nonmanager facilitates a small meeting. The people frankly discuss and evaluate issues about their culture and values.[17]

8. _____ Journals and Values: At Customlink, new employees are given journals. They are asked to record instances when company values are enacted and also questions they might have. At the end of the month, they meet and discuss how to live company values.[18]

9. _____ Whistle Blowing Hotline: Xerox has a strong internal whistleblower program with a 24/7 multilingual global hotline. This prevents the buildup of unethical practices and reassures employees of the company's commitment to their well-being.[19]

10. _____ Letters to Loved Ones: At Pepsico, the CEO writes letters to the spouses and parents of her people and identifies the wonderful contributions they have made in the past year.[20]

SEEING POSSIBILITY

Based on the following scale, indicate your interest in each of these practices.

Uninterested 1 2 3 4 5 6 7 8 9 10 Interested

1. _____ Outside Thought Leaders: Kimberly-Clark understands the value of learning from other organizations. They recruit a group of "thought leaders" from other companies and from universities and think tanks for one day per year to collaborate and join in innovative dialogue.[21]

2. _____ Creating Purpose and Passion: To unify the VW brand, the CMO learned German; interviewed 100 staff; traveled the globe to discover shared, key points of pride; used wide involvement to create a centralized brand; and tied it to the points of pride.[22]

3. _____ Paradigm Change: Walgreens moved beyond the drugstore concept. This was accomplished through a 12-week "Well Experience" Field Training effort that includes a simulated store and innovative training techniques. After the training, customer satisfaction went up.[23]

4. _____ Global Excellence: IKEA works to have high standards globally. If, for example, there is a demanding new law passed in one country, stores and suppliers in all countries comply.[24]

5. _____ Open Innovation: Medtronic engages in an "open innovation" strategy. They invite and facilitate contributions from companies, customers, and universities to help solve problems and assist in generating products. They even created a web portal to encourage the process.[25]

6. _____ External Sharing-Learning: The Motley Fool is an investment firm that holds a monthly Workplace Foolosophy Tour. Outsiders learn of the practices that support the positive culture. The visitors are also invited to share their ideas.[26]

7. _____ Spreading Excellence: Humana employs three people with the responsibility to visit all areas, look for excellence, and then find ways to move the patterns of excellence across the company.[27]

8. _____ Cross Silo Sharing: At Plains All American Pipeline, employees make occasional "day in the life" presentations that allow

colleagues from different departments a glimpse into the work of a separate division.[28]

9. _____ Crossing the Bridge: At DaVita, executives use many "traditions and symbols" to facilitate organizational change. For example, as a new employee begins to believe in the values of the company, the employee is recognized and celebrated for having "crossed the bridge."[29]

10. _____ Accelerator Experiences: Procter & Gamble puts future leaders into small businesses with great strategic potential. They seek to make the experience as discontinuous as possible so as to accelerate learning and growth.[30]

EMBRACING THE COMMON GOOD

Based on the following scale, indicate your interest in each of these practices.

Uninterested 1 2 3 4 5 6 7 8 9 10 Interested

1. _____ Pursuing the Highest Good: Whole Foods has a Declaration of Interdependence. The objective is to align and pursue the best interests of all stakeholders so everyone wins all the time.[31]

2. _____ Productivity Games: The German software company SAP uses games to keep the atmosphere upbeat and productive. The game "SAP Vampire Hunt" encourages employees to identify energy wasters; in return, they earn points and save energy for the company.[32]

3. _____ Caring for the Whole: Robert W. Baird & Co. has a "no assholes policy." They value doing things the "right way, all the time," and they have extreme on-boarding and mentoring policies designed to socialize people into their highly cohesive and caring culture.[33]

4. _____ Ego Management: At Goldman Sachs, first-person singular is only used to describe a mistake and not accomplishments. For example, instead of using "I," a banker would say "We secured a big trade." This "pronoun education" puts an emphasis on teamwork and ego management.[34]

5. _____ Shaping the Future Together: At Conductor, everyone gets to help shape the future. Once a year, all employees spend a day in self-

organized teams. It is called Hack Day. The teams develop ideas to improve the product, their office, or the company as a whole.[35]

6. _____ Mentor Recognition: Accenture's People Developer department allows promoted employees to name colleagues who helped them along the way, and the efforts of these helpers are recognized by company leaders.[36]

7. _____ Participation in Big Moments: Cirque du Soleil wants every person to "feel the magic" of creating the ultimate show. So, at the start of every new show, all employees are invited to participate in raising the big top.[37]

8. _____ Weekly Celebrations: MindValley is a digital publishing firm. They hold a weekly meeting called the Awesomeness Report. With music playing, they celebrate the accomplishments of the past week and build off the enthusiasm to establish big goals for the coming week.[38]

9. _____ Making the Mission Real: Toms is a shoe company with a social mission. They give shoes away in 28 countries where having shoes helps prevent a number of diseases. After employees have worked for Toms for a year, they are invited to go to other countries and help distribute shoes. Doing so makes the company's mission and values real.[39]

10. _____ Positive Tickets: In Richmond, Canada, the Mounted Police addressed a spiraling youth crime rate with a novel idea—giving "positive tickets" to youth they discovered doing a good thing for the community; these tickets entitled them to free entry at the movies or a youth center. Crime statistics were greatly reduced.[40]

TRUSTING THE EMERGENT PROCESS

Based on the following scale, indicate your interest in each of these practices.

Uninterested 1 2 3 4 5 6 7 8 9 10 Interested

1. _____ Eliminating Bureaucracy: Instead of giving new employees a handbook of policies, Quicken Loans seeks out their ideas on how the business could run better. They deemphasize bureaucracy and encourage empowerment.[41]

2. _____ Servant Leadership: People at The Motley Fool refer to the organization as a "low-rarchy." This is a reminder that everyone is a leader and senior people exist to serve the needs of their associates throughout the organization.[42]

3. _____ Idea Market: Rite-Solutions puts new product ideas into an internal marketplace. Each idea begins trading at $10. Each employee has $10,000 of play money to invest. Employees can also sign up to work on a proposed project. If an idea turns into a real product, play money can be redeemed for cash.[43]

4. _____ Decentralization of Innovation: Amazon seeks to decentralize innovation. All new job candidates are asked what they have invented. Most employees are given innovation challenges. Teams are taught how to experiment and create.[44]

5. _____ Job Crafting: At Burt's Bees, employees are encouraged to rewrite their job descriptions to better fit their personal motives and strengths.[45]

6. _____ Shared Business Plan: SC Johnson trusts every employee with a 50-page overview of their business objectives and personalizes each copy with the employee's name.[46]

7. _____ Leader Selection: A primary reason people leave companies is dissatisfaction with supervision. At W. L. Gore and Associates, units are comprised of approximately 10 people, and leaders are elected from within the team.[47]

8. _____ Culture Fit: Instead of carrying out performance evaluations, managers at Zappos do culture assessments and give employees feedback on how they fit within the culture and can better support it.[48]

9. _____ Vacation Time: Talent Plus is a consulting firm that emphasizes trust over control. There is no limit on vacation time, and associates are encouraged to take days as needed. Most people take no more than 10 days.[49]

10. _____ Creative Conversations: Salesforce encourages dialogue about ideas. Employees are awarded points for producing an idea, commenting on another's, or receiving a comment on theirs. Meaningful ideas and contributions are rewarded.[50]

ADDITIONAL POSITIVE PRACTICES

Based on the following scale, indicate your interest in each of these practices.

Uninterested 1 2 3 4 5 6 7 8 9 10 Interested

1. _____ Diversity Appreciation: Marriott International recognizes the importance of diversity. The company hosts an Associate Appreciation Week, in which a day is used to appreciate cultures and backgrounds of employees.[51]

2. _____ Culture Service Training: Zappos is a culture-focused company. They give new employees five weeks of training on things like core values and customer service.[52]

3. _____ Space Design: At CBRE in Los Angeles, no workspaces are assigned to individuals. People select from 15 different kinds of space designs to fit the needs of the moment.[53]

4. _____ Career Banding: Mercedes Benz uses career banding—a strategy that consolidates narrow job grades into fewer bands with wider salary ranges. This facilitates cross-training and career movement within the company, and presents employees with new opportunities, as well.[54]

5. _____ Fun: Make-A-Wish Foundation is serious about fun. The CEO is the "Fairy Godmother of Wishes." Meetings have candied themes, and the office is full of toys.[55]

6. _____ Spot Bonuses: At NetApp, exceptional individual or team performance is rewarded with a "spot" bonus. The process has a positive effect, and the number of bonuses has increased from year to year.[56]

7. _____ Profitability Training: Keller Williams Realty has a training program for agents to increase profitability. For seven weeks, there is intense pursuit of leads and business growth opportunities. There is continuous emphasis on mindset, language, and techniques and big results. Graduates of this program increased their closed transactions by 50 percent and increased their income by 114 percent.[57]

8. _____ Focus on Customer Satisfaction: Prudential Real Estate has shifted its client satisfaction data. They put less emphasis on

low scores and focus instead on high scores and what they can learn from satisfied customers. As a result, both employee and customer satisfaction scores have increased.[58]

9. _____ Team Camps: Hilti Corporation continually immerses employees in the company culture. They hold "Team Camps" every 12 to 18 months, and employees attend the camps in a location away from their office. They focus on teamwork and core values.[59]

10. _____ Pay to Quit: Amazon has a "Pay to Quit" policy. The objective is to make it easier for uncommitted people to leave. People are offered $2,000 to leave the first year, and the amount goes up to $5,000 in the fourth year.[60]

11. _____ Living Close to Work: At the Motley Fool, they adopted a value that every employee should make enough to afford to live close to the place of employment. This led them to increase the pay of the lowest 10 percent.[61]

12. _____ Pre-Mortem Risk Evaluations: McCarthy Building Companies, a commercial contractor company, organizes "Pre-Mortem" sessions to recognize likely, high-impact risks and take proactive actions to mitigate them. Much money has been saved through this practice.[62]

13. _____ Eliminating Waste: Mohawk Industries invested in Waste Stream Management Training to eliminate all waste from manufacturing facilities. The program has saved the company millions of dollars and now extends to other recyclables.[63]

14. _____ Skill Recognition Levels: La Quinta is passionate about having clean hotel rooms. It has developed a Heart of the House certification program with various "belts," much like in martial arts. As skills improve, employees get higher degree belts.[64]

15. _____ Updates on Strategy: The CEO of Twitter provides constant updates on the strategy and progress of the company so all employees are fully informed as to where the organization is headed.[65]

16. _____ Book Club: Mercedes Benz Financial Services has a book club. Executives discuss how a book has influenced their career or life. This contributes to both professional development and relationship building.[66]

17. _____ Skip-Level Meetings: Intel focuses on being open and approachable to employees. Management actively carries out "Skip-Level One on Ones" to hear the opinions of staff and work to actively address those issues.[67]

18. _____ Weekly Video: At New York Life Insurance, the CEO distributes a weekly video. It updates people on key recent activities and offers encouragement on the week ahead.[68]

19. _____ Making Values Real: Prologis specifies six core values and is particularly careful to live them during the worst of times. Such integrity makes the values real. People begin to believe in them and live by them. It gives rise to a culture of commitment.[69]

20. _____ Transformation: Sonic Automotive has changed car buying. Employees empower customers to own the process. Stressful negotiations are eliminated. Customers are given accurate data, and pricing is based on the data. Market share is increasing.[70]

21. _____ Genuine People Investing: Starbucks has rolled out a "Starbucks College Achievement Plan" that provides employees a financial incentive to obtain a college degree. This is a genuine investment in its people, and employees are not required to remain with the company after completing their education.[71]

22. _____ Peer Recognition: At Wegmans Food Markets, employees are able to recognize and reward one another with gift cards paid for by the company.[72]

23. _____ Learning from the Past: Toyota has a robust mentorship system within the company, even for top-level executives. Current company executives are paired with retired ones, and this helps upper management learn from the past and better plan for the future.[73]

24. _____ Customer Retention: If Zappos is out of a desired product, employees help customers obtain the product from a competitor. This surprising level of service contributes to high customer retention.[74]

25. _____ Celebrate Retirees: SC Johnson makes a point to celebrate retirees. Each one receives an Award of Appreciation and a special celebration is held. They receive lifetime medical and dental benefits, and have lifetime access to company facilities.[75]

26. _____ A Central Culture Symbol: Plante Moran believes they can win by having a uniquely caring culture. The central concept is the golden rule, and every employee has a golden ruler on their desk.[76]

27. _____ Empowerment: Intel puts emphasis on safety. The value is so strong, employees feel empowered to stop the flow of work if they feel something is unsafe or unclear.[77]

28. _____ Gratitude Wall: The City of Ballarat in Victoria, Australia, maintains a Gratitude Wall. Employees' record their appreciation for the things they value in their personal and professional lives.[78]

29. _____ Board Representation: The Neutral Zone is a highly success-ful program for youth in Ann Arbor, MI. The 29-person board in-cludes 13 youth who have full involvement in and influence on high-level decisions. They are treated like adults.[79]

30. _____ Cocreation: At Menlo Innovations Software Factory, all programming is done in pairs. This unusual practice of cocreat-ing software promotes an energized learning culture, and many benefits accrue.[80]

31. _____ Work-Life Balance: American Express encourages work-life balance. Many associates work from home, and the additional flex-ibility in their schedule has allowed them to dedicate themselves fully in both their personal and work lives.[81]

32. _____ Red Zone Reports: The Boston Consulting Group advocates work-life balance. They issue "red zone" reports to identify em-ployees who have registered too many hours on a given project.[82]

33. _____ Sabbaticals: Autodesk, a software developer, encourages its employees to go on sabbaticals (six weeks of paid time off every four years). This offers an opportunity to travel or spend quality time with friends and family, while simultaneously getting well-deserved rest and relaxation.[83]

34. _____ Banking Overtime Hours: Freese and Nichols allows employees to bank their overtime hours into personal leave. This allows people to leave work to attend to things like their children's activities.[84]

35. _____ Concierge Service: Bronson Healthcare sees employees as whole people, and they have a concierge service that helps employ-ees with personal problems that may emerge during the day.[85]

36. _____ Higher Pay: At Costco, employees are paid more than at peer companies. The belief is that it is more profitable to reduce turnover and stimulate productivity, commitment, and loyalty than to minimize pay.[86]

37. _____ Crisis Fund: Mercy Health has an employee-generated crisis fund that people may tap into in times of financial emergency.[87]

38. _____ Investing in People: When the recession hit, Ernst & Young did the opposite of other companies. They increased hiring and invested in training, engagement, and culture development. This eventually led to a 30 percent growth trajectory.[88]

39. _____ Transitions: Qualcomm often does mergers and acquisitions. An employee experience team works with the newcomers to make them feel welcomed and to ease their sense of transition. They also recognize and adopt positive office traditions from the former company.[89]

40. _____ Fun Bunch: Instead of having management plan bonding activities, Alliance Data Systems has a group called the "Fun Bunch"—a group of associates that take charge of team-bonding activities.[90]

41. _____ Recognizing Service: Marriott has a "Spirit to Serve Award." When an associate is positively singled out by a guest, the person gets a certificate. Each time this happens, a gold bar is added to the certificate.[91]

42. _____ Newsletter: Accenture has an online newsletter that carries stories of employee accomplishments outside of work. Others may post their comments and messages of congratulations.[92]

43. _____ Product Quality: At Amazon, customer service officers are able to pull a product back from sale if they have received multiple complaints from customers.[93]

44. _____ Innovation Protection: Walmart accelerated its innovation efforts by establishing an "idea incubator" and protected the effort from the bureaucracy by locating it in Silicon Valley rather than at the headquarters in Arkansas.[94]

45. _____ Peer Review: At W. L. Gore and Associates, pay and promotion is determined by peers, who rate each unit member on the impact the person made on the enterprise.[95]

46. _____ Global Colleague Finding: Carswell has an employee directory called "Colleague Finder." Associates can search for others around the world, based on personal and professional interests. This helps employees connect in meaningful ways and promotes a global mindset across the business.[96]

47. _____ Integrating Remote People: Staff.com is an online company with employees who work remotely. They have implemented a Video Game Day in which all employees play online together. This gets around the lack of interaction and has helped with interdivision communication.[97]

48. _____ Exceptional Employees: The Cheesecake Factory has a "Scoops Live" website that allows everyone to share and comment on company news, videos, and stories about exceptional employees.[98]

49. _____ Culture Committee: At Southwest Airlines, they believe their culture is a competitive advantage, and there is an elected committee of 96 employees responsible for the vitality of the culture.[99]

50. _____ Alumni Relations: J.P. Morgan has an Alumni Relations Group that stays in touch with ex-colleagues. In addition, it allows the company to "boomerang" hire (rehire people who have left). This further strengthens the culture and cuts costs for the company.[100]

Step Four
Selecting Your Practices
My Plan for Creating a More Positive Culture

Now consider the vision you wrote in Step 1. See if any of practices you are most interested in will help you to achieve your vision. Choose three to six that you feel will help you most in creating a more positive organization. Record them below.

Positive Practices

1.

2.

3.

4.

5.

6.

Step Five
Writing Customized Practices
My Plan for Creating a More Positive Culture

Now examine the aforementioned practices and reinvent them to fit your situation. You should create approximately three to six practices according to the following criteria:

- Each reinvented practice fits your specific situation.
- You believe that each reinvented practice will work.
- The prospect of implementing the practice excites you.
- You can implement the practice without asking permission.

When you are done, print this page, and put it somewhere that will help you keep them top of mind.

My Customized Practices   **Start Date**

1.

2.

3.

4.

5.

6.

▲ NOTES

Introduction

1. In 2003, Kim Cameron, Jane Dutton, and I published a book called *Positive Organizational Scholarship: Foundations of a New Discipline*. It was a call for academics to study individuals, groups, and organizations at their very best. Since then, the field has come into its own, and many scholars do research on the topic. In 2012, Kim Cameron and Gretchen Spreitzer published *The Oxford Handbook of Positive Organizational Scholarship*, which contains more than 80 chapters of scientific literature reviews and illustrates how much the field has grown. The central hub for this global research network is the Center for Positive Organizations at the University of Michigan's Ross School of Business. The Center for Positive Organizations encourages research, develops applied tools, works with companies to improve their culture, and provides educational experiences for students. See Kim S. Cameron, Jane Dutton, and Robert E. Quinn (Eds.), *Positive Organizational Scholarship: Foundations of a New Discipline* (San Francisco: Berrett-Koehler, 2003); and Kim S. Cameron and Gretchen M. Spreitzer (Eds.), *The Oxford Handbook of Positive Organizational Scholarship* (Oxford: Oxford University Press, 2012), http://positiveorgs .bus.umich.edu/.

2. The central question of this book is how to embrace and act from the positive mindset so as to create a more positive or excellent organization. In a recent book, Sutton and Rao address the same question: they ask how constructive beliefs can be spread from the few to the many, and they show how to build and uncover pockets of excellence in an organization. Their book takes a different approach but is a very useful supplement to this one. In terms of leadership, Kim Cameron has written two books that articulate positive strategies and practices. Both books supplement this one nicely, as well. See Robert I. Sutton and Huggy Rao, *Scaling Up Excellence: Getting to More without Settling for Less* (New York: Crown Business, 2014); Kim S. Cameron, *Positive Leadership: Strategies for Extraordinary Performance*, 2nd ed. (San Francisco: Berrett-Koehler, 2012); and Kim S. Cameron, *Practicing Positive Leadership: Tools and Techniques That Create Extraordinary Results* (San Francisco: Berrett-Koehler, 2013).

Jane Dutton and Gretchen Spreitzer have also produced a very helpful volume; see Jane E. Dutton and Gretchen M. Spreitzer (Eds.), *How to Be a Positive Leader: Insights from Leading Thinkers on Positive Organizations* (San Francisco: Berrett-Koehler, 2014).

Chapter 1

1. The tendency to defend our beliefs is called the "confirmation" or "my side" bias. Research suggests that we look for, interpret, and remember information that supports what we already believe. See Jonathan Baron, *Thinking and Deciding*, 3rd ed. (New York: Cambridge University Press, 2000), 203.

2. Carol Dweck's research may support the existence of this third orientation. Dweck finds that some managers have what she calls a "growth mindset." They believe that people can learn and change, and this belief leads these managers to behave differently. They are more likely to persist to win-win outcomes, more open to discussion, more willing to forgive and forget, more oriented to challenging and developing people, more likely to reinforce the successes of their people, and have more zest for teaching. In other words, they have very positive mental maps. See Carol S. Dweck, *Mindset: The New Psychology of Success* (New York: Ballantine Books, 2006).

3. Normal either/or thinking processes cause us to evaluate leaders in one of two ways: as task oriented or as people oriented. Studies of transformational leadership regularly show that effective leaders are bilingual—that is, they are high on both task and person. Because this both/and orientation violates our normal either/or categories, it is difficult to see; even experts took years to notice the patterns in front of them. Leaders who are more behaviorally complex, or bilingual, have been shown to be more effective generally. See K. Lawrence, P. Lenk, and R. E. Quinn, "Behavioral Complexity in Leadership: The Psychometric Properties of a New Instrument to Measure Behavioral Repertoire," *The Leadership Quarterly* 20, no. 2 (2009): 87–102; and C. A. Schriesheim, R. J. House, and S. Kerr, "Leader Initiating Structure: A Reconciliation of Discrepant Research Results and Some Empirical Tests," *Organizational Behavior and Human Performance* 15, no. 2 (1976): 297–321.

4. Figure 1.1 is constructed using the logic of competing values. The logic results in a conceptually balanced perspective. A positive characteristic is located (Full engagement). The question is asked, what would it mean to take this positive characteristic too far (Exhaustion)? With the positive and negative in mind, a search is made for a second positive characteristic (Life balance). It must be a positive version of the negative that has been identified (Exhaustion). It must also have a negative extension (Withdrawal) that contrasts with the existing positive opposition (Full engagement). Other applications of competing values logic can be found in the following book. See Kim S. Cameron, Robert E. Quinn, Jeff DeGraff, and Anjan V. Thakor, *Competing Values Leadership: Creating Value in Organizations* (Edward Elgar Publishers, Northhampton, MA, 2006).

5. F. Scott Fitzgerald, "The Crack Up," *Esquire* magazine (Feb., March, Apr., 1936).

6. Research suggests that positive individual behaviors predict organization performance, and as positive practices increase, performance increases. Outcome measures include productivity and financial performance. From the study of nursing units, Cameron

and his colleagues concluded: "Improvement in patient satisfaction, internal climate, employee participation, and quality of care occurs when organizations provide compassionate support for employees, emphasize positive and inspiring messages to employees, forgive mistakes, express gratitude to and confidence in employees, clarify the meaningfulness of the work being done, and reinforce an environment characterized by respect and integrity. No one positive practice stands out as the single most important determinant of improvement, but positive practices in combination appear to have the most powerful impact." See Kim S. Cameron, Carlos Mora, Trevor Leutscher, and Margaret Calarco, "Effects of Positive Practices on Organizational Effectiveness," *Journal of Applied Behavioral Science* 47, no. 3 (2011): 266–308.

Chapter 2

1. Tables 2.1 and 2.2 articulate some of the differences between conventional assumptions and positive assumptions. The top portion of each table derives from a conversation with publisher Steve Piersanti. The bottom portion, listing the assumptions of what people will do, are adapted from a literature review on positive change. See Robert E. Quinn and Ned Wellman, "Seeing and Acting Differently: Positive Change in Organizations," in Kim S. Cameron and Gretchen M. Spreitzer (Eds.), *The Oxford Handbook of Positive Organizational Scholarship* (Oxford: Oxford University Press, 2012).

2. Jim Collins and Jerry I. Porras, *Built to Last: Successful Habits of Visionary Companies* (New York: Harper Business, 1994).

3. Books like *Built to Last* are often criticized from two perspectives. First, companies that are defined as excellent may subsequently fall on hard times, and critics suggest that they were not excellent after all. This criticism assumes that excellence is a fixed condition, and to achieve it is to never fail. If, on the other hand, excellence can be seen as a complex, dynamic, and temporary state that derives from constant learning and adaptation, and failure does not indicate that the company was not excellent at the earlier time. The second criticism is that if no systematic comparison is made with other organizations, it is impossible to know if the identified, exemplary characteristics are really the differentiators that account for success.

4. Research on prosocial goals suggests that many companies have prosocial purpose statements but there is no impact on the way people in the organization actually behave. A purpose statement can be comprised of empty words, or the statement may have been valid in the past but not the present. In some cases, the statement can be an authentic purpose that is understood, accepted, and followed by employees. See Julian Birkinshaw, Nicolai J. Foss, and Siegwart Lindenberg, "Combining Purpose with Profits," *Sloan Management Review*, Spring 2014, http://sloanreview.mit.edu/article/combining -purpose-with-profits.

Chapter 3

1. A higher purpose is "an intent, perceived as producing a social benefit over and above the monetary payoff shared by the employer and employee." A mathematical model of higher purpose in organizations suggests that when an organization is imbued with an authentic, higher purpose, conventional assumptions of transaction are

transcended, and people work harder for the same financial incentives. See Robert E. Quinn and Anjan V. Thakor, "Imbue the Organization with a Higher Purpose," in Jane E. Dutton and Gretchen M. Spreitzer (Eds.), *How to Be a Positive Leader: Insights from Leading Thinkers on Positive Organizations* (San Francisco: Berrett-Koehler, 2014), 100–11.

2. Vaill argued that the definition and clarification of purpose is evident in all the high-performing systems. It emerges from a constant stream of management actions. Self-promoting executives who are "just passing through" are unlikely to clarify and communicate a meaningful purpose. Wanting an outcome for the organization "cannot be faked." In every word and behavior, executives communicate what they really want. Employees know. People of purpose care deeply about the organization, they become invested in the culture, and they see the purpose as something that has intrinsic value. The leader is "in the system and the system is in the leader." These leaders know what is important and are not distracted by the chaos that is found in every organization. They focus themselves and others on what is important. Imbuing an organization with purpose provides guidance while allowing freedom to act. The people can experiment and learn their way forward. From this forward movement and constant learning, the newest form of the organization emerges. The movement and learning is not linear. The organization is not a machine; it is a social system that continually reinvents itself. See Peter Vaill, "The Purposing of High-Performing Systems," *Organizational Dynamics* (Autumn 1982): 23–39.

3. At the highest level of moral influence is the transcendence of self-interest. Positive leaders transcend self-interest, focus on the common good, and model altruism and other virtues. Because they strive to live by social ideals, they attract others to do the same. This kind of power is called "idealized influence." It invites others to dedicate themselves to the common good. See Bernard M. Bass, *Transformational Leadership: Industry, Military and Educational Impact* (Mahwah, NJ: Lawrence Erlbaum Associates, 1998), 165.

Chapter 4

1. P. Block, "Foreword," in Roger Harrison (Ed.), *A Consultant's Journey: A Dance of Work and Spirit* (San Francisco: Jossey-Bass, 1997).

2. Alex (Sandy) Pentland, *Honest Signals: How They Shape Our World* (Cambridge, MA: MIT Press, 2008).

3. Bruce J. Avolio, Jakari Griffith, Tara S. Wernsing, and Fred O. Walumbwa, "What Is Authentic Leadership Development?" in P. Alex Linley, Susan Harrington, and Nicola Garcea (Eds.), *The Oxford Handbook of Positive Psychology at Work* (Oxford: Oxford University Press, 2010), 39–52.

Chapter 5

1. In one of his books, Weinzweig provides a document on how to share the Zingerman's experience. It comes from their staff handbook and includes eight pages of guiding principles. A person seeking to build a positive organization could benefit from reading and translating the principles from the food business to any organization. See

Ari Weinzweig, *A Lapsed Anarchist's Approach to Building a Great Business* (Ann Arbor, MI: Zingerman's Press, 2010), 325–32.

2. The comments here refer to two papers that appeared in the *Harvard Business Review*. The first suggests that there is a conventional or normal state and that there is the fundamental state of leadership. In the normal state, we tend to be comfort centered, externally directed, self-focused, and internally closed. This is our natural condition, and we spend much time in it. We can also self-elevate. We can become results centered, internally directed, other-focused, and externally open. In this condition, our influence greatly increases. One way to think about the fundamental state of leadership is to examine our own moments of greatness. In them, we can see what it meant to be results centered, internally directed, other-focused, and externally open. See Robert E. Quinn, "Moments of Greatness: Entering the Fundamental State of Leadership," *Harvard Business Review* (July–August 2005): 75–83.

For a more comprehensive treatment on how to use the concept, see Ryan W. Quinn and Robert E. Quinn, *Lift: The Fundamental State of Leadership*, 2nd ed. (San Francisco: Berrett-Koehler, 2015).

The second paper is called "How to Play to Your Strengths." It assumes that we may grow more if we develop our gifts and leverage our natural strengths. It provides a method called the "Best Self Exercise." In the exercise, you obtain feedback from people who know you best. Instead of articulating your weaknesses, the respondents identify your greatest strengths and ground them by sharing short stories of when you were at your very best. By reflecting on past manifestations of your best self, you can increase the probability of bringing forth your best self in the present. You can become proactive about it. See Laura Morgan Roberts, Gretchen Spreitzer, Jane Dutton, Emily Heaphy, Brianna Barker, and Robert E. Quinn, "How to Play to Your Strengths," *Harvard Business Review* (January 2005): 75–80.

3. The notion of using excellence to challenge the conventional mental map takes root in the method known as "appreciative inquiry." The assumption is that organizations emerge from conversations, and new and better ways of organizing are limited by the lack of imagination. Appreciative inquiry avoids problem solving. It orients people to appreciating the best of what is, envisioning what might be possible, holding conversations about what should emerge, and then moving toward the creation of what will be. See D. L. Cooperrider and S. Srivastava, "Appreciative Inquiry in Organizational Life," in R. W. Woodman and W. A. Pasmore (Eds.), *Research in Organizational Change and Development*, vol. 1 (Stamford, CT: JAI Press, 1987), 129–69.

Chapter 6

1. H. D. Thoreau, "Civil Disobedience," originally published in 1849, published in *Civil Disobedience and Other Essays* (New York: Dover, 1993), 1–18.

2. At the highest level of moral influence is the transcendence of self-interest. Positive leaders transcend self-interest, focus on the common good, and model altruism and other virtues. Because they strive to live by social ideals, they attract others to do the same. This kind of power is called "idealized influence." It invites others to dedicate themselves to the common good. See Bernard M. Bass, *Transformational Leadership:*

Industry, Military and Educational Impact (Mahwah, NJ: Lawrence Erlbaum Associates, 1998), 165.

3. Adam M. Grant and Justin Berg, "Prosocial Motivation at Work: When, Why, and How Making a Difference Makes a Difference," in Kim S. Cameron and Gretchen M. Spreitzer (Eds.), *The Oxford Handbook of Positive Organizational Scholarship* (Oxford: Oxford University Press, 2012), 29.

4. Ibid.

5. Otto Scharmer and Katrin Kaufer, *Leading from the Emerging Future: From Ego-System to Eco-System Economies* (San Francisco: Berrett-Koehler, 2013).

6. Robert E. Quinn, Gretchen M. Spreitzer, and Jerry Fletcher, "Excavating the Paths of Meaning, Renewal and Empowerment: A Typology of Managerial High Performance Myths," *Journal of Management Inquiry* 4, no. 1 (1995): 16–39.

7. Normal either/or thinking processes cause us to evaluate leaders as being task or people oriented. Studies of transformational leadership show that effective leaders are bilingual. That is, they are high on both task and person. Because this both/and orientation violates our normal either/or categories, it is difficult to see. Leaders who are more behaviorally complex, or bilingual, have been shown to be more effective. See K. Lawrence, P. Lenk, and R. E. Quinn, "Behavioral Complexity in Leadership: The Psychometric Properties of a New Instrument to Measure Behavioral Repertoire," *The Leadership Quarterly* 20 no. 2 (2009): 87–102; and C. A. Schriesheim, R. J. House, and S. Kerr, "Leader Initiating Structure: A Reconciliation of Discrepant Research Results and Some Empirical Tests," *Organizational Behavior and Human Performance* 15, no. 2 (1976): 297–321.

Chapter 7

1. The Gandhi account is adapted from one of my earlier books. See Robert E. Quinn, *Change the World: How Ordinary People Can Achieve Extraordinary Results* (San Francisco: Jossey-Bass, 2000), 144–91.

2. Ibid. The account of the CEO is adapted from the same book.

3. Heifetz differentiates between technical problems and adaptive problems. Technical problems tend to be easy to identify and lend themselves to the quick solutions of an expert; solutions are implemented in a straightforward manner and are less likely to be resisted. Adaptive problems are difficult to identify and are often denied because they require a change in values, beliefs, roles, relationships, and approaches. The people with the issue are the ones who end up working on it. The work often requires cooperation across boundaries. Solutions require trial and error experiments leading to new discoveries. Implementation takes a long time and cannot be accomplished through administrative commands. Resistance is common. Heifetz suggests five principles to help people do adaptive work.

- Identify the adaptive challenge. Diagnose the situation in light of the values at stake, and unbundle the issues that come with it.
- Keep the level of distress within a tolerable range for doing adaptive work. To use the pressure cooker analogy, keep the heat up without blowing up the vessel.
- Focus attention on ripening issues and not on stress-reducing distractions. Identify which issues can currently engage attention; while directing attention to them, counteract work avoidance mechanisms like denial, scapegoating, externalizing

the enemy, pretending the problem is technical, or attacking individuals rather than issues.

- Give the work back to people, but at a rate they can stand. Place and develop responsibility by putting the pressure on the people with the problem.
- Protect voices of leadership without authority. Give cover to those who raise hard questions and generate distress—people who point to the internal contradictions of the society. These individuals often will have latitude to provoke rethinking that authorities do not have. See R. A. Heifetz, *Leadership without Easy Answers* (Cambridge, MA: Harvard University Press, 1994), 128.

4. The warehouse account is adapted from *Change the World*. The case originally appeared in Joel Youngblood's *Life at the Edge of Chaos: Creating the Quantum Organization* (Dallas: Perceval, 1997), 13.

5. Ibid. The account of the classroom exercise is adapted from the same book.

6. This story is paraphrased from an account by Kurt Wright. See Kurt Wright, *Breaking the Rules: Removing the Obstacles to Effortless High Performance* (Boise, ID: CPM Publishing, 1998), 9–10.

7. The emergent process is associated with complexity theory. In nature, collections of interacting units may have the capacity to evolve as a whole system. Without any central coordinating mechanism such as a leader or a plan, the collective may begin to self-organize and transform. Individual agents act on a local basis, and the acts are represented and communicated through the network of agents or units. Multiple agents may represent multiple options. Some of the options are adopted by the whole. See Mary Uhl-Bien and Russ Marion, "Introduction: Complexity Leadership—A Framework for Leadership in the Twenty-First Century," in Mary Uhl-Bien and Russ Marion (Eds.), *Complexity Leadership, Part 1: Conceptual Foundations* (Charlotte, NC: Information Age Publishing: 2008), xii.

8. The action box integrates the work of Heifetz (see note 3 on technical versus adaptive problems) and the material in this text.

Chapter 8

1. Positive Leadership™ The Game is an interactive card game designed for leaders of all levels. It helps players generate innovative solutions to business problems through structured brainstorming. Played in groups of three to ten people, this game uses the underlying principles of positive organizations to spark multiple strategies for leading positive change and development. The game is available at the Center for Positive Organizations at: http://positiveorgs.bus.umich.edu/cpo-tools/positive-leadership-the -game/.

Appendix

1. Tim Goshert, "The Power of a Clear, Concise Vision," Reliable Plant, September 2006, http://www.reliableplant.com/Read/2432/power-of-a-clear,-concise-vision.

2. "Leading in the 21st Century: An Interview with Ford's Alan Mulally," McKinsey & Company, November 2013, http://www.mckinsey.com/insights/strategy/leading_in_the _21st_century_an_interview_with_fords_alan_mulally.

3. James R. Bradley, "Bridging the Cultures of Business and Poverty," *Stanford Social Innovation Review*, Spring 2003, http://www.ssireview.org/articles/entry/bridging_the_cultures_of_business_and_poverty.

4. Sammyclem, "Food with Integrity: How Chipotle Maintained Growth, Improved Values, and Silenced the Critics," *Business, Society, and Government 4*, November 11, 2012, http://bizgovsoc4.wordpress.com/2012/11/11/food-with-integrity-how-chipotle-maintained-growth-improved-values-and-silenced-the-critics/.

5. Conference Proceedings, http://rossmedia.bus.umich.edu/rossmedia/Play/cc7e84a6e80748b0b1d9695c4ca236d61d?catalog=6feb0db7-e845-4144-90b5-6747bcde50a0.

6. FedEx Website, http://about.van.fedex.com/fedex-cares-week.

7. Doug Conant, "Why Philanthropy Is R&D for Business," McKinsey & Company, September 2013, http://www.mckinsey.com/insights/corporate_social_responsibility/why_philanthropy_is_r_and_d_for_business.

8. Josh Bersin, "New Research Unlocks the Secret of Employee Recognition," *Forbes*, June 13, 2012, http://www.forbes.com/sites/joshbersin/2012/06/13/new-research-unlocks-the-secret-of-employee-recognition/.

9. "Top Ten People Practices from the 2012 Best Small & Medium Workplaces List," http://www.greatplacetowork.com/storage/documents/publications/top-ten-people-practices.pdf.

10. Conference Proceedings, http://rossmedia.bus.umich.edu/rossmedia/Play/cc7e84a6e80748b0b1d9695c4ca236d61d?catalog=6feb0db7-e845-4144-90b5-6747bcde50a0.

11. Quality Feedback, http://www.ey.com/Publication/vwLUAssets/Outperforming_the_competition/$FILE/Outperforming_the_competition.pdf.

12. Leigh Buchanan, "How Kimpton Hotels Scaled Its Culture," *Inc.*, March 2014, http://www.inc.com/magazine201403/leigh-buchanan/kimpton-hotels-culture.html.

13. Ari Weinzweig, "Ten Rules for Great Finance," Zingerman's Website, http://www.zingtrain.com/node/101.

14. Michael Burchell and Jennifer Robin, "How to Build It, How to Keep It, and Why It Matters," Great Place to Work, http://www.thegreatworkplaceonline.com/bestpractices.html.

15. Todd Henneman, "DreamWorks Animation Cultivates a Culture of Creativity," *Workforce*, August 4, 2012, http://www.workforce.com/articles/dreamworks-animation-cultivates-a-culture-of-creativity.

16. Michigan Ross Positive Business Conference, "Positive Business Awards," 2014, http://positivebusinessconference.com/sessions/positive-business-awards/.

17. "Top Ten People Practices from the 2012 Best Small & Medium Workplaces List," http://www.greatplacetowork.com/storage/documents/publications/top-ten-people-practices.pdf.

18. "Top Ten People Practices from the 2012 Best Small & Medium Workplaces List," http://www.greatplacetowork.com/storage/documents/publications/top-ten-people-practices.pdf.

19. "Highlights of Select Winners from the 2012 World's Most Ethical Companies," *Ethisphere*, June 4, 2013, http://ethisphere.com/magazine-articles/highlights-of-select-winners-from-the-2012-worlds-most-ethical-companies/#sthash.CN4UlDGY.Fx2U6UTJ.dpuf.

20. Andy Serwer, "(Say Wha???) The CEO Who Writes Her Employees' Parents," *Fortune*, January 28, 2014, http://fortune.com/2014/01/28/say-wha-the-ceo-who-writes -her-employees-parents/.

21. Soren Kaplan, "4 Innovation Strategies from Big Companies That Act Like Start- ups," *Fast Company*, http://www.fastcodesign.com/1670960/4-innovation-strategies -from-big-companies-that-act-like-startups.

22. Ilan Mochari, "The Misunderstood Art of Leading an Innovative Culture," *Inc.*, http://www.inc.com/ilan-mochari/linda-hill-purpose-driven-leadership-innovation.html.

23. "Training Top 125," *Training*, January/February 2014, 10, http://www.trainingmag .com/sites/default/files/2014_01_Training_Top_125_1.pdf.

24. IKEA Group, "How We Manage Sustainability in Our Business," http://www.ikea .com/ms/en_US/pdf/sustainability_report/group_approach_sustainability_fy11.pdf.

25. Katharine Grayson, "Medtronic Seeks Ideas with New Web Portal," *Minnea- polis/St. Paul Business Journal*, January 21, 2011, http://www.bizjournals.com/twincities /print-edition/2011/01/21/medtronic-seeks-ideas-with-new-web.html?page=all.

26. Scicotello, "*First Friday Workplace Foolosophy Tour*," Best Places to Work, No- vember 26, 2012, http://culture.fool.com/2012/11/26/lets-talk-culture-come-to-our -first-friday-freefurall/.

27. Shared in a personal communication with the author.

28. Erin Mulvaney, "No. 3 Large Company: Plains All American Pipeline," *Chron*, November 7, 2013, http://www.chron.com/business/top-workplaces/article/No-3-large -company-Plains-All-American-Pipeline-4936518.php.

29. "Kent Thiry and DaVita: Leadership Challenges in Building and Growing a Great Company," *Stanford Graduate School of Business* OB.54 (2006): 1–28. Print. https://hbr.org/product/kent-thiry-and-davita-leadership-challenges-in-bui/an/OB54 -PDF-ENG.

30. Patricia O'Connell, "How Companies Develop Great Leaders," *Bloomberg Busi- ness*, February 16, 2010, http://www.businessweek.com/stories/2010-02-16/how -companies-develop-great-leadersbusinessweek-business-news-stock-market-and -financial-advice (accessed February 19, 2015).

31. Whole Foods Website, http://www.wholefoodsmarket.com/mission-values/core -values/declaration-interdependence.

32. M. Herger, "Gamifying Sustainability @ SAP," SAP Community Network, Sep- tember 30, 2011, http://scn.sap.com/people/mario.herger/blog/2011/09/30/gamifying -sustainability-sap (accessed February 19, 2015).

33. Great Place to Work/Great Rated! Website, "Robert W Baird & Co.," http://us .greatrated.com/robert-w-baird-co.

34. "Leadership Development at Goldman Sachs," *Harvard Business School* 002nd ser. 9.406 (2007): 1–23. Print. https://hbr.org/product/Leadership-Development-at/an /406002-PDF-ENG.

35. "Top Ten People Practices from the 2012 Best Small & Medium Workplaces List," http://www.greatplacetowork.com/storage/documents/publications/top-ten-people -practices.pdf.

36. "25 Best Global Companies to Work For," *Fortune,* October 2011, http://money .cnn.com/galleries/2011/fortune/1110/gallery.best_companies_global.fortune/21 .html.

37. "Cirque du Soleil," *Harvard Business School* 006th ser. 9.403 (2002): 1–12. Print. https://hbr.org/product/cirque-du-soleil/403006-PDF-ENG.

38. Kira M. Newman, "4 Keys to Mindvalley's Quirky, Driven Company Culture," Tech Cocktail Kuala Lumpur, June 11, 2012, http://www.finerminds.com/career -entrepreneurship/a-day-in-the-life-of-mindvalley/ and http://tech.co/mindvalley-culture -2012-06.

39. Tamara Schweitzer, "The Way I Work: Blake Mycoskie of Toms Shoes," *Inc.*, http://www.inc.com/magazine/20100601/the-way-i-work-blake-mycoskie-of-toms -shoes.html.

40. "Cops Give Out Positive Tickets," Good News Network, October 6, 2013, http:// www.goodnewsnetwork.org/cops-in-canada-giving-out-positive-tickets/.

41. "Quicken Loans: Enduring an Entrepreneurial Spirit," *Ross School of Business* 760th ser. 1.428 (2009): 1–5. Print. http://ref.michigan.org/cm/attach/7D12A0E2-EC21 -487D-B52F-B6E78698C571/Quicken%20Loans%20case%20study.pdf.

42. http://rossmedia.bus.umich.edu/rossmedia/Play/cc7e84a6e80748b0b1d9695c4 ca236d61d?catalog=6feb0db7-e845-4144-90b5-6747bcde50a0.

43. Jay Rao and Joseph Weintraub, "How Innovative Is Your Company's Culture?" *MITSloan Management Review Magazine*, Spring 2013, http://sloanreview.mit.edu /article/how-innovative-is-your-companys-culture/.

44. Jeff Dyer and Hal Gregerson, "The Secret to Unleashing Genius," *Forbes*, August 14, 2013, http://www.forbes.com/sites/innovatorsdna/2013/08/14/the-secret-to -unleashing-genius/.

45. Jane Dutton, "Job Crafting at Burt's Bees," *GlobaLens*, November 2009, http:// globalens.com/casedetail.aspx?cid=1428854.

46. Great Place to Work, Best Practices, http://www.greatplacetowork.ie/best-practices.

47. Gary Hamel, "Innovation Democracy: W. L. Gore's Original Management Model," Management Innovation Exchange, September 23, 2010, http://www .managementexchange.com/story/innovation-democracy-wl-gores-original-management -model.

48. Susan M. Heathfield, "20 Ways Zappos Reinforces Its Company Culture," About Money, http://humanresources.about.com/od/organizationalculture/a/how-zappos -reinforces-its-company-culture.htm.

49. Great Place to Work/Great Rated! Website, "Talent Plus," http://us.greatrated .com/talent-plus.

50. https://help.salesforce.com/HTViewHelpDoc?id=ideas_reputation.htm &language=en_US.

51. Great Place to Work/Great Rated! Website, "Marriott International," http://us .greatrated.com/marriott-international-inc.

52. Joe Gerard, "Best Practices in Corporate Culture: Zappos," i-Sight, http://i-sight .com/best-practice/best-practices-in-corporate-culture-zappos/.

53. BD+C Staff, "CBRE's Bold Experiment: 200-person Office with No Assigned Desks," Building Design + Construction, October 31, 2013, http://www.bdcnetwork .com/cbres-bold-experiment-200-person-office-no-assigned-desks-slideshow.

54. Michael Burchell and Jennifer Robin, "How to Build It, How to Keep It, and Why It Matters," Great Place to Work, http://www.thegreatworkplaceonline.com/best practices.html.

55. Adam Grant and Lauren Malcolm, "Serious Play at the Make-A-Wish Foundation," GlobaLens, October 2009, http://globalens.com/casedetail.aspx?cid =1428873.

56. Great Place to Work/Great Rated! Website, "NetApp," 2015, http://us.greatrated .com/netapp.

57. "Training Top 125," *Training*, January/February 2014, http://www.trainingmag .com/sites/default/files/2014_01_Training_Top_125_1.pdf.

58. Cameron Plews, "Positive Leadership in Action: Applications of POS by Jim Mallozzi, CEO, Prudential Real Estate and Relocation," *Organizational Dynamics*, (2012), http://www.langleygroup.com.au/images/Cameron—Plews—2012— Positive-leadership-in-action-copy.pdf.

59. "Select Best Practices from the World's Best: Cisco: Appreciating Coworkers with the Click of a Button," http://www.greatplacetowork.com/best-companies/worlds-best -multinationals/best-practices.

60. Chris Isidore, "Amazon Offers Employees $5,000 to Quit," *CNN Money*, http:// money.cnn.com/2014/04/11/technology/amazon-pay-to-quit/.

61. Liz Stiverson, "Culture and Purpose Are Their Own Reward: Tom Gardner," Wharton Forum, Work/Life, http://worklife.wharton.upenn.edu/2014/08/culture -purpose-reward-tom-gardner-motley-fool/.

62. "Training Top 125," *Training*, January/February 2014, http://www.trainingmag .com/sites/default/files/2014_01_Training_Top_125_1.pdf.

63. Ibid., 4.

64. Ibid., 40.

65. Jacquelyn Smith, "The Best Companies to Work for in 2014," *Forbes*, December 11, 2013, http://www.forbes.com/sites/jacquelynsmith/2013/12/11/the-best -companies-to-work-for-in-2014/2/.

66. "Top Ten People Practices from the 2012 Best Small & Medium Workplaces List," http://www.greatplacetowork.com/storage/documents/publications/top-ten-people -practices.pdf.

67. Michael Burchell and Jennifer Robin, "How to Build It, How to Keep It, and Why It Matters," Great Place to Work, http://www.thegreatworkplaceonline.com/best practices.html.

68. "Midsize No. 3: Employees Give New York Life Insurance a Big F—and That's Good," *Dallas Morning News*, November 8, 2013, http://www.dallasnews.com/business /top-100/headlines/20131108-midsize-no.-3-employees-give-new-york-life-insurance -a-big-f—and-thats-good.ece.

69. Mike Kacsmar, "Flexibility, Transparency, and Values Drive Entrepreneur's Success," *Forbes*, May 28, 2014, http://www.forbes.com/sites/ey/2014/05/28/flexibility -transparency-and-values-drive-entrepreneurs-success/.

70. "Training Top 125," *Training*, January/February 2014, http://www.trainingmag .com/sites/default/files/2014_01_Training_Top_125_1.pdf.

71. Luci Scott, "Starbucks Offers Workers Free College Tuition," *USAToday*, June 16, 2014, http://www.usatoday.com/story/news/nation/2014/06/16/starbucks-free-college -tuition/10569971/ (accessed February 19, 2015).

72. Erica D Hawan, "5 Best Companies for Engagement," August 22, 2013, http:// ericadhawan.com/5-best-companies-employee-engagement/.

73. Deryl Sturdevant, "(Still) Learning from Toyota," McKinsey & Company, February 2014, http://www.mckinsey.com/insights/manufacturing/still_learning_from _Toyota.

74. 'Tunde Olanrewaju, Kate Smaje, and Paul Willmott, "The Seven Traits of Effective Digital Enterprises," McKinsey & Company, May 2014, http://www.mckinsey.com /insights/organization/the_seven_habits_of_highly_effective_digital_enterprises.

75. Michael Burchell and Jennifer Robin, "How to Build It, How to Keep It, and Why It Matters," Great Place to Work, http://www.thegreatworkplaceonline.com/best practices.html.

76. "Plante Moran: All You Really Need to Know," *Ross School of Business* 579th ser. 1.428 (2009): 1–7. Print. http://globalens.com/DocFiles/PDF/cases/Preview/GL1428 759P.pdf.

77. Great Place to Work/Great Rated! Website, "Intel Corporation," http://us .greatrated.com/intel-corporation.

78. Garry Davis, CoB Positive Business Project, http://www.youtube.com/watch?v =hgT8-ubW69M.

79. http://rossmedia.bus.umich.edu/rossmedia/Play/f6073c5706c64561a0ed81464 883393b1d?catalog=6feb0db7-e845-4144-90b5-6747bcde50a0.

80. Thomas Meloche, James Goebel, and Richard Sheridan, "Paired Programming in the Software Factory: Q&A," The Menlo Institute, 2003, http://www.menloin novations.com/by-reading/PDF/paired_programming_q_and_a.pdf.

81. Great Place to Work/Great Rated! Website, "American Express," http://us .greatrated.com/american-express.

82. Meg McSherry Breslin, "Part of Boston Consulting Group's Success Comes from Looking Out for Its Workers," *Workforce*, February 20, 2013, http://www.workforce .com/articles/part-of-boston-consulting-group-s-success-comes-from-looking-out-for -its-workers.

83. Great Place to Work, http://www.greatplacetowork.net/best-companies/worlds -best-multinationals/profiles-of-the-winners/1531-10-autodesk.

84. Tanya Rutledge, "No. 5 Small Company: Freese and Nichols," *Chron*, November 7, 2013, http://www.chron.com/business/top-workplaces/article/No-5-small-company -Freese-and-Nichols-4936614.php.

85. Susan Ulshafer, Marilyn Potgeisser, and Tillie Hidalgo Lima, "Concierge Services Help Deliver Better Work/Life Balance at Bronson Healthcare Group," InvenZone, *Journal of Organizational Excellence*, 2005, http://www.invenzone.com/research _papers/concierge-services-help-deliver-better-work-slash-life-balance-at-bronson -healthcare-group-22619943.

86. Tim Worstall, "Of Course Costco Supports a Higher Minimum Wage: It Already Pays Above It," *Forbes*, March 6, 2013, http://www.forbes.com/sites/timworstall /2013/03/06/of-course-costco-supports-a-higher-minimum-wage-it-already-pays -above-it/.

87. Arkansas Business Staff, "Employee Fund Is Fundamental at Mercy Health," September 23, 2013, http://www.arkansasbusiness.com/article/94713/employee-fund-is -fundamental-at-mercy-health.

88. Tiffany Barber, "Spotlight on Ernst & Young: Transforming Your Company Culture during Challenging Times," Great Place to Work, May 9, 2012, https://www .greatplacetowork.com/publications-and-events/blogs-and-news/996#.U4UwoS_rExU.

89. Great Place to Work/Great Rated! Website, 2015, http://us.greatrated.com /qualcomm.

90. "Annual 'Mothership Tour' Takes Alliance Data Systems Boss to Every Location," *Dallas Morning News*, November 8, 2013, http://www.dallasnews.com/business /top-100/headlines/20131108-midsize-winner-annual-mothership-tour-takes-alliance -data-systems-boss-to-every-location.ece.

91. Jessica Rohman, "Developing Recognition Practices that Strengthen Company Culture," Great Place to Work, August 14, 2013, http://www.greatplacetowork.net /publications-and-events/blogs-and-news/1742-developing-recognition-practices-that -strengthen-company-culture.

92. Michael Burchell and Jennifer Robin, "How to Build It, How to Keep It, and Why It Matters," Great Place to Work, http://www.thegreatworkplaceonline.com/best practices.html.

93. Marc Onetto, "When Toyota Met E-Commerce: Lean at Amazon," McKinsey & Company, February 2014, http://www.mckinsey.com/insights/operations/when _toyota_met_e-commerce_lean_at_amazon.

94. Kim Souza, "Wal-Mart Presence Grows in Silicon Valley with New Tech Center," *The City Wire*, March 26, 2014, http://www.thecitywire.com/node/32346# .U7MOhi_rExU.

95. "Best Companies 2014," *Fortune*, http://fortune.com/best-companies/w-l-gore -associates-22/.

96. Michael Burchell and Jennifer Robin, "How to Build It, How to Keep It, and Why It Matters," Great Place to Work, http://www.thegreatworkplaceonline.com/best practices.html.

97. Ilya Pozin, "15 Crazy Company Culture Perks that Paid Off," LinkedIn, April 22, 2014, http://www.linkedin.com/today/post/article/20140422154219-5799319-15 -crazy-company-culture-perks-that-paid-off.

98. Great Place to Work/Great Rated! Website, "Cheesecake Factory," http://us .greatrated.com/cheesecake-factory.

99. Dick Ambrosius, "Do You Have the Power of Purpose?" *Grand Lifestyle*, April 28, 2014, http://www.grandmagazine.com/news/2014/04/power-purpose/.

100. Chris van Mossevelde, "8 Benefits of Social Media Use for Talent Management," *Universum*, November 12, 2013, http://universumglobal.com/2013/11/8-benefits -of-social-media-use-for-talent-management/#ixzz34kJmcpNU.

▲ INDEX

▲ ABOUT THE AUTHOR

Shauri Quinn Dewey

When Robert E. Quinn was in college, he was trying to decide what to major in. After much soul-searching, he came to an unusual conclusion. He decided to major in change. The only problem was that there was no major in change. So he had to become a proactive consumer of education and pursue possibility in the midst of constraint. Since then, he has studied change, taught change, and consulted on change. He is currently the Margaret Elliott Tracy Collegiate Professor in the Management and Organization Group at the University of Michigan's Ross School of Business. He is one of the cofounders of the Center for Positive Organizations at the Ross School. At the Center, he delights in learning from his colleagues who are working to understand and create organizations in which people flourish and exceed expectations. He has published 16 books, including *Beyond Rational Management; Deep Change; Change the World; Building the Bridge as You Walk on*

It; *Diagnosing and Changing Organizational Culture* (with Kim Cameron); *Lift: The Fundamental State of Leadership* (with Ryan Quinn); *The Deep Change Field Guide*; and *The Best Teacher in You* (with Kate Heynoski, Michael Thomas, and Gretchen Spreitzer), which was winner of the Ben Franklin Award, best education book for 2015. Bob has been married to his wife, Delsa, for 45 years. They have six children and fifteen grandchildren who continue to remind him of the importance of pursuing possibility in the midst of constraint.

Berrett–Koehler
Publishers

Connecting people and ideas
to create a world that works for all

Dear Reader,

Thank you for picking up this book and joining our worldwide community of Berrett-Koehler readers. We share ideas that bring positive change into people's lives, organizations, and society.

To welcome you, we'd like to offer you a free e-book. You can pick from among twelve of our bestselling books by entering the promotional code **BKP92E** here: http://www.bkconnection.com/welcome.

When you claim your free e-book, we'll also send you a copy of our e-newsletter, the *BK Communiqué*. Although you're free to unsubscribe, there are many benefits to sticking around. In every issue of our newsletter you'll find

- A free e-book
- Tips from famous authors
- Discounts on spotlight titles
- Hilarious insider publishing news
- A chance to win a prize for answering a riddle

Best of all, our readers tell us, "Your newsletter is the only one I actually read." So claim your gift today, and please stay in touch!

Sincerely,

Charlotte Ashlock
Steward of the BK Website

Questions? Comments? Contact me at bkcommunity@bkpub.com.